SAPPERS

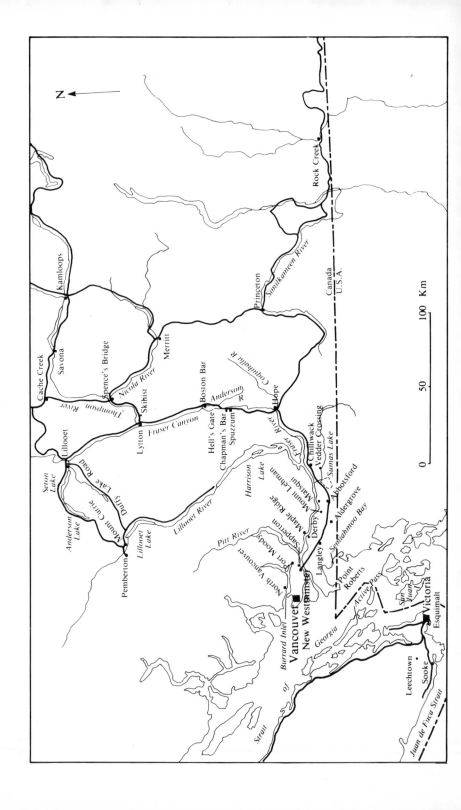

SAPPERS

The Royal Engineers in British Columbia

Beth Hill

Horsdal & Schubart

Horsdal & Schubart Publishers Ltd.
Box 1
Ganges, BC
V0S 1E0

Cover painting by Rex Woods, "Cariboo Road", courtesy of Confederation Life Insurance Company, Toronto, Ontario

Maps by Peggy Ward, North Vancouver, BC

Chapter-head drawings by Tim Williamson, Ganges, BC

Design and typesetting by The Typeworks, Vancouver, BC. This book is set in Janson.

Printed and bound in Canada by Hignell Printing Limited, Winnipeg, Manitoba.

The publisher is grateful to acknowledge that this publication has been financially assisted by the Government of British Columbia through the British Columbia Heritage Trust.

Canadian Cataloguing in Publication Data

Hill, Beth, 1924-
Sappers

Bibliography: p.
Includes index.
ISBN 0-920663-05-2

1. Great Britain. Army. Corps of Royal Engineers - History. 2. British Columbia - History - 1849-1871.* I. Title.
FC3822.9.R6H54 1987   971.1'02   c86-091568-9
F1088.H54 1987

Contents

Acknowledgements

When I was a child in Ontario, my father taught me history; here the Fenians occupied a ridge, or this was the road Laura Secord walked, he would tell me, and we often detoured to examine some old grave. Now, in my adopted province, I still ask who lived here before me. Landscape without history is as sterile as history removed from landscape. Therefore I have happily explored southern British Columbia in research for this book, and this land now has new and fascinating dimensions for me. So that others may share this experience, I have ended the book with a list of sites associated with the Sappers.

This account of the Royal Engineers in British Columbia is necessarily brief; it is not the definitive history of the Sappers and I trust will not be judged as such. That history will presently be written by the acknowledged authority, Frances Woodward, who kindly took the time to read my manuscript. I am also indebted to John Spittle for his advice and critical reading of the manuscript. Many people have assisted me; though I cannot mention them all, I would like to give special thanks to Provincial Archivist John A. Bovey for permission to quote from documents in the Provincial Archives, and to the staff of that excellent institution. I am grateful to Archie Miller of Irving House, the custodians of St. Mary's Sapperton, Herbert Haskin of the Museum of the Royal Westminster Regiment, Zane Lewis of the BC Provincial Museum, Mrs. M. E. Hall of Chilliwack, Lorraine Harris, Dr. George Stanley for permission to quote extensively from his book *Mapping the Frontier*, David Suttill of the Heritage Conservation Branch, and Mrs. J. H. Hamilton. As always, I've been accompanied and encouraged by my husband, Ray Hill, and my friend, Shirley Sexsmith. The work of the young artist, Tim Williamson, adds much to the appearance of the book. Confederation Life graciously gave permission for the use of the painting on the cover: "Cariboo Road", by Rex Woods.

Beth Hill

Introduction

Unaware, British Columbians walk with the ghosts of the Royal Engineers. Lying like the fingers of a hand across the Lower Mainland, the roads laid out by the Engineers, now called South Marine Drive, Kingsway, Canada Way, North Road and Pitt River Road, carry modern traffic. Along the streets of New Westminster, Hope, Yale and Lillooet, their horses and mules plunged through the spring mud. They came in 1858, the year when 30,000 gold seekers flooded up the valley of the Fraser River; when the gold rush was over, a few of the miners and most of the Royal Engineers chose to stay, to live out their lives as pioneer settlers. They held a vision of a land of peace and plenty, without poverty, without the horrors of Dickens' England. When the Colonial Secretary of 1858, Sir Edward Bulwer Lytton, dispatched the first contingent of Royal Engineers to what is now British Columbia, he told them,

> You go not as enemies but as the benefactors of the land
> you visit, and children unborn will, I believe, bless the
> hour when Queen Victoria sent forth her sappers and
> miners to found a second England on the shores of the Pacific.[1]

Modern British Columbians, Lytton's "children unborn",
are, for the most part, unacquainted with the debt they owe
the sappers and miners. If asked about the Royal Engineers,
they usually associate them, quite correctly, with the building
of the Cariboo Road. Rarely do they know more. Yet this
small group of men, about 200 in all, arriving in the years of
crisis when the pattern of the colony's future was abruptly
forged, played an important role in the dramatic events of
their time and helped to shape the province British Columbians now inhabit. Those who know the story of the sappers
also understand British Columbia.

The Royal Engineers have always been an elite corps; the
word "engineer" originally designated a person skilled in the
art of constructing defences, more gifted than others, perhaps
a genius, or *génie*, as the French still call their engineers. In the
Bayeux Tapestry, Humphrey de Tilleul, possibly the first
Royal Engineer, is seen constructing a fort to be transported
by sea from Normandy to England in prefabricated sections.
If mediaeval fortress defenders could not be starved into submission, the attackers had to break down the wall either by
tunnelling underneath or by battering; the man with the
shovel was the sapper. The origin of the word "sap" is obscure
but it apparently refers not only to the vital juice of plants but
also to some kind of spade or mattock.

The amazing galleries and tunnels of Gibraltar are the work
of English engineers. Before 1772, the Gibraltar works were
executed by civilian tradesmen who could quit when they
didn't want to work. "Not being amenable to military dis-

cipline, they were indolent and disorderly and wholly regard-
less of authority."[2] To eliminate this intolerable degree of
freedom, the Soldier Artificer Company was organized, consisting of non-commissioned officers and privates skilled as
stone-cutters, smiths, gardeners, carpenters, etc. In 1797 the
original Soldier Artificers were absorbed into a larger Corps
of Royal Military Artificers, at this time abandoning their
scarlet uniforms. The red jackets were restored in 1813 when
the sappers fought in the Battle of Waterloo. Eleven companies of Royal Sappers and Miners took part in the Crimean
War. Out of a force of 935 (all ranks) in the Crimea, there
were 445 casualties; modern warfare had begun. In 1856 the
Corps of Sappers and Miners was incorporated into the Corps
of Royal Engineers, thus ending the strange arrangement of
having the military engineer officers and soldiers in separate
corps. What is a sapper? "He is a man of all work of the Army
and the public—astronomer, geologist, surveyor, draughts-
man, artist, architect, traveller, explorer, antiquary, me-
chanic, diver, soldier and sailor; ready to do anything or go
anywhere; in short, he is a Sapper."[3] The Royal Engineers
performed in most of these roles in British Columbia, but
their achievements were more than the sum of their activities.

The list of duties above does not include being a spy but the
first Royal Engineers to arrive on the west coast were spies. In
1845, Lieutenant Mervin Vavasour and Lieutenant Henry
James Warre were sent in the guise of sportsmen to the
Oregon Territory (then part of the British Empire) to examine
the military feasibility of defending it against the Americans.
Vavasour had been in Canada since 1841, working on the
canals in Upper Canada.

It is perhaps in the nature of espionage that the importance
of the Warre and Vavasour expedition is uncertain. One his-
torian has written that their report "influenced the decision
which settled on the 49th parallel as our boundary, but pre-
serving Vancouver Island intact in British territory."[4]

"You will be careful to preserve perfect secrecy as to the objects of the journey which you are to undertake," warned

Lieutenant Vavasour's commanding officer. "Proceed ostensibly in the capacity of a private individual, seeking amusement, but you will examine well the more important parts of the country referred to, so as to guide the prosecution of military operations, should such operations become necessary."[5] These apparent tourists, Fort Victoria's first important visitors, did not impress the Hudson's Bay men there— "the fur-traders formed a low estimate of their character and abilities"[6]—but perhaps their conclusions concerning the difficulty of holding the Columbia, once it had been settled by Americans, were realistic.

Vavasour and Warre travelled from the Red River valley to the Columbia, leaving on June 16, 1845 and arriving at Fort Colville on August 16. From the journey of 62 days they concluded that the route was impracticable for the transport of troops. Maintaining their disguise sometimes made it difficult for them to make adequate surveys and sketches, but their report is nevertheless comprehensive, detailed and thorough.

The fear of an expensive and difficult war with the United States led Britain to accept the extension to the Pacific Ocean of the boundary line along the 49th parallel, with only Vancouver Island remaining British territory to the south of this line. The Oregon Boundary Treaty was signed on June 15, 1846. It was easy to draw the boundary line with a ruler straight across a map. Marking this line on the earth's surface across two ranges of towering mountain peaks defended by mosquitoes was work of a different order, and for this work the British government turned, of course, to the Royal Engineers.

Chapter One

1858: The Boundary Commission

The 1818 agreement between the United States and Great Britain, which had made the 49th parallel the boundary from the Great Lakes only as far as the Rocky Mountains, did not address the question of Oregon. The aggressive young American nation, delighted with the idea that it was their "manifest destiny" to expand to the Pacific Ocean, was determined to possess the Columbia River area, called the "Oregon Territory". As its claim to the Oregon Territory was weak historically, and as the British fur traders were already established there, the American government encouraged American settlers to simply move in and take possession. The success of this policy was demonstrated by the Oregon Boundary Treaty of 1846, which gave Oregon to the United States and set the 49th parallel as the boundary.

However, it was not until the first rumours of gold discoveries reached ears in London and Washington that the two
governments did anything about determining where, exactly,
the 49th parallel lay. Both nations appointed commissions in
1857, the American Boundary Commission landing in Victoria on June 22, 1858. It was headed by Archibald Campbell,
who was inclined to be "stiff to the point of inflexibility."[1]
The American party moved to Point Roberts to determine, by
astronomical observations, the starting point of the boundary
line. The British Boundary Commission had sailed from
Southampton almost two months earlier, on April 2, 1858,
for the West Indies, where some members became ill with
yellow fever. After crossing the Isthmus of Panama by train,
they came north in the *Havannah*, most of those ill with fever
recovering *en route*. They arrived at the entrance of the Strait
of Juan de Fuca on July 11.

> We entered the straits which are about 12 miles broad at 6
> in the morning & were lucky enough to have a very fine
> day. Thousands of puffins kept flying across our bow
> reminding one very much of home. The scenery going up
> the straits is perfectly lovely, alternately beautiful glades
> with trees scattered about, the very facsimile of an English
> park & the dark forests of gigantic pines, cedars & firs,
> whilst in the background you can see the Cascade Moun-
> tains, with their snowy heads. We came along with a
> splendid breeze.[2]

Charles Wilson, Royal Engineer, secretary of the British
Boundary Commission, recording his excitement upon entering the Strait of Juan de Fuca was actually looking at the
Olympic Mountains, not the Cascades. Also aboard the
Havannah was his commanding officer, Lieutenant-Colonel
John Summerfield Hawkins, R.E.; the success of the joint
venture would require his skill and patience in negotiations
with his intransigent American colleague Archibald Campbell. The others were there too: astronomers Captain C. J.

Darrah, R. E. and Captain R. E. Haig, R.A., surgeon and naturalist Dr. David Lyall, R.N., naturalist and veterinary surgeon J. K. Lord, geologist Dr. Hilary Bauerman, and 56 non-commissioned officers and sappers. When the work was completed Lord wrote a guidebook for prospective immigrants to the area and both Lyall and Bauerman wrote serious scientific studies. However, it is the journal of Charles Wilson, written for the amusement of his sister Fanny, that gives the richest account of the work of the Royal Engineers of the Boundary Commission.

George F. G. Stanley, the editor of Charles Wilson's diary, commented that the document reflects the man himself, "an academic dilettante in red tunic and epaulets,"[3] and asked that Wilson's class and generation be considered, when he at times

Officers of the Boundary Commission. Standing (l. to r.): Lieutenant Anderson, RE; Colonel Hawkins, RE; Lieutenant Wilson, RE. Sitting (l. to r.): Captain Darrah, RE; Mr. Lord; Captain Haig, RA.

appeared somewhat conceited and patronizing. Certainly his later military career, crowned by a knighthood bestowed by Queen Victoria, demonstrated his ability. Deciding to be a soldier, Wilson placed second out of 46 candidates in the competitive examinations and in 1855 received a commission in the Royal Engineers. The scribbled notes of this intelligent, energetic young man give lively views of the work of surveying and marking the boundary. He also learned the Chinook language and wrote a useful treatise about the life of the Indian people he encountered.

> July 12th. As soon as possible we landed and set off along the trail to Victoria & found it a wonderful place, all the miners for an immense distance round the fort in tents, they are the finest collection of men I ever saw together, all in the full blow of manhood & the finest specimens of nearly every race on earth, English, American, French, German, Spanish, Chinese with their queer looking eyes, Sandwich Islanders & dusky Indians with their painted faces; as you may imagine where there is so much young blood & no female population there are sometimes fierce scenes enacted & the bowie knife & revolver which every man wears are in constant requisition, but up to this time very few fatal cases have occurred.

> July 13th. This morning I went on shore with Darrah to stroll along the shore of the harbour. We felt just like schoolboys out for a holiday after our long imprisonment of 70 days on board ship.... Vancouver Island is most beautiful, but turned quite upside down by the gold discovery, a regular San Francisco in '49.[4]

Vancouver Island was an infant colony; the first immigrants, 18 men, had only arrived in 1849, just ahead of their first governor. Eighty more came in 1850 and the next year brought 140. They found accommodation and food in short supply, for workmen had flocked to find gold in California.

The new immigrants were usually unprepared for the rough life. "Scarcely anyone remembered to bring such everyday necessities as needles and thread".[5] By 1857, there were about 400 adults in Fort Victoria.

They feared the Indians. Vavasour and Warre made a list of the tribes of the Oregon Territory and stated that there were 75,868 individuals in the tribes where a census had been made and another 11,079 where no census had been taken. The British Columbia Indian population of 1835 is estimated to have been 70,000. A night watch was kept at the fort, but the 18-foot cedar wall must have seemed a mere picket fence when stories were told of the fierce Cowichans a few miles to the north.

The man who slept inside the palisade, on whom the settlers relied and against whom they continually railed— "Old Square-toes", they called him—was James Douglas, Governor of the Colony of Vancouver Island, Chief Factor of the Hudson's Bay Company, Agent of the Puget's Sound Agricultural Company, Land Agent of the Hudson's Bay Company, a bulldog of a man who kept the area British in spite of the invasion of 30,000 gold seekers in 1858. One evening in 1857, after dinner in the Mess Hall of the fort, he pulled from his pocket a small bag containing a few grains of scale gold from the North Thompson River. He remarked casually that he "thought it meant a great change and a busy time."[6] The residents of Victoria were just leaving church on a Sunday morning in April 1858, when the American side-wheel steamer *Commodore* entered the harbour. Astounded, they watched about 450 men disembark, more than doubling the population of the town. The gold rush had begun.

Lieutenant Richard Charles Mayne, R.N., who had served on the northwest coast since 1857 aboard the survey vessel H.M.S. *Plumper*, returned to Esquimalt from surveying in the San Juan Islands in May, a month after the first gold seekers arrived,

to find that during our absence that most infectious of all

maladies—a gold-fever—had broken out, and had seized
every man, woman and child there and in Victoria. Everyone, whom a few weeks ago we had left engaged steadily in
pursuits from which they were reaping a slow sure profit,
seemed to have gone gold-mad.... The excitement of Victoria was indescribable.... The value of land was raised
immensely.... Merchants' stores were rising in every
direction. On the shore of the harbour, wharves were being
planted... sailing-ships, laden with every description of
articles which a migratory population could, and in many
cases could not, want, flowed into the harbour. Victoria
appeared to have leapt at once from the site of a promising
settlement into a full-grown town.... Expectation was
written on every face.[7]

The Royal Engineers of the Boundary Commission arrived
in July, three months after the first gold seekers. Charles Wilson recorded that,

You are hardly safe without arms & even with them, when
you have to walk along paths across which gentlemen with
a brace of revolvers each are settling their differences; the
whiz of revolver bullets round you goes on all day & if anyone gets shot of course it's his own fault; however I like the
excitement very much & never felt better in my life. All the
worst characters of the coast are crowding here in thousands, though only a month has elapsed since the discovery
of gold, they have exported 8000 oz. from Victoria alone &
reports from the mines of the mainland say they will far
outrival the San Francisco ones.[8]

After a day of walking about dodging bullets, young
Lieutenant Wilson settled to his duties, shared a conference
with Captain James Charles Prevost, R.N., the English commissioner responsible for determining the water boundary between the mainland and Vancouver Island, and made arrangements to move the Royal Engineers to quarters prepared for

Victoria Harbour and James Bay, 1860. *An engraving for Mayne's book based on a water colour by Sarah Crease.*

them at Esquimalt. He also walked to Victoria and interviewed the Hudson's Bay men about provisions.

> Our house is situated in a beautiful place, in 50 yrds walk you get right into the dense forest; as there is only room in the house for the officers, the men are all under canvas. Dr. Lyall, our surgeon and Botanist, joined us today. We are all roughing it here, there was nothing in the house but bare walls, or rather wood with sun dry crevices through which daylight is visible; there is not such a thing as a brick or stone house in the Island, all being of wood, so we are lucky in getting this.[9]

It was not only Wilson who felt like a schoolboy when he came ashore at Esquimalt; the Royal Engineers kicked up their heels as well:

> July 19th. Last night we had our first great row: on coming back in the evening, I found nearly half the men absent &

COURTESY OF PROVINCIAL ARCHIVES OF BC

in a short time some came in who said they had seen some
lying drunk in the road & that there had been some fighting
between our men & some Americans up at Victoria so we
rigged ourselves out with a dark lantern, bowie knife, cut &
thrust sword and a revolver each and took a strong picquet
out. After tumbling over stumps & wandering through the
woods in the dark from 9 till 2 in the morning (by a very
slight road & that only passed over twice before) we managed to bring back all except two, who came in next day.
Great excuses must be made for the men on their first
holiday after over 100 days at sea on salt meat & they now
continue to go on quite steadily & dont show any symp-
toms of bolting to the mines.[10]

Arriving from San Francisco with some of the first miners,
a well-to-do merchant named Alfred Waddington commented
that "Never perhaps was there so large an immigration in so
short a space of time into so small a place."[11] Without police or
regular soldiers, Governor Douglas was faced with a new and
dangerous situation. Only three weeks after the arrival of the
Royal Engineers, they were called to help him keep the peace.
Charles Wilson wrote in his diary:

July 31st. Last night we were roused up by a message from
the Governor to say that a riot had broken out at Victoria,
& our presence was instantly required. The men were soon
turned out & got on board the *Plumper* (one of our Men of
War here) which carried us around. It was very exciting
when we came in sight of the town & the order was given to
load & the ship's guns run out & cleared for action; we had
to disembark in boats & if there had been any resistance
there would have been very few of us not knocked over.
Luckily however we found that after rescuing a prisoner &
knocking over the sheriff, the mob had dispersed. However
our work was not all finished as we had to search some of
the ships & get back the prisoner, which we succeeded in
doing, with four of the ringleaders in the rescue, without

much resistance. After this the Governor gave us a good supper, & we then had a dreary march home at 5 in the morning, not blessing the authorities for calling us up during the night.[12]

The next morning, Mr. Campbell, the American commissioner, arrived and it was decided that the astronomers should go over to the mainland with a party of men to begin work. That evening they all went to a ball given by the officers of the *Plumper* where they met the young ladies of Vancouver Island. Wilson noted that two of the Misses Douglas "had just had some hoops sent out to them & it was most amusing to see their attempts to appear at ease in their new costume."[13]

Wilson was responsible for the work of 56 non-commissioned officers and sappers. Including the seven officers, the number of men involved was increased to about 125 when packers, woodsmen and guides were hired. The Americans also found it necessary to have four companies of infantry to protect them from the Indians, a service the British did not require.

The first lengthy discussions between the two comissioners took place in August at Semiahmoo Bay. Hawkins thought the work should include cutting the boundary line so that there was a vista through the trees, with numerous permanent iron markers, whereas Campbell, considering Hawkins's plan too expensive, advocated markers at a few established points. The question was not finally resolved until a meeting at Fort Colville in November 1860, when Campbell agreed that the boundary west of the Cascades should be marked with iron monuments, paid for by the British government. The British team had, in the meantime, been cutting a vista along the line. Perhaps the harmonious achievements of the joint commission may be attributed to the fact that the two groups worked independently and rarely met.

On August 26, 1858, Haig, Darrah and Lyall set off up the Fraser River with some of the sappers to establish a camp at Sumas Lake. A few days later, the Royal Engineers were again called into action by Governor Douglas. As large numbers of miners had moved into Indian lands, it is not surprising that there were conflicts between the two groups.

In June 1858 Douglas had hurried to Yale where the Indians were threatening to attack the miners. He lectured both miners and Indians, warning them that the laws would protect the rights of both. When he returned to Victoria, Douglas wrote to the Colonial Secretary of the danger of an Indian war. In July one battle occurred near Boston Bar when a group of miners was able to beat off an attack. "In addition, smaller groups of miners were on several occasions ambushed and many individuals lost their lives."[14] The miners, under an American, Captain H. M. Snyder, organized a force of 167 men and negotiated treaties with the Indians, an admirable achievement, given the usual American view that the only good Indian was a dead one. Receiving the first incorrect reports of a bloody battle on August 29, Douglas took the military force available to him, 35 Royal Engineers and some marines, and hurried again to Yale.

Charles Wilson wrote:

August 30th. In consequence of the very bad reports from the mines up Fraser river, Major Hawkins has gone up with a body of men, to help the Governor to keep the peace. I volunteered several times to go up as a little fighting would be much more to my taste than this work; but unfortunately being a Jack-of-all-trades & having most of the work to do, I was left behind much to my sorrow. I am very anxious for news from the party, as there has been a good deal of fighting up there & wise heads in these matters say we are going to have a regular Indian war. If so it will knock the Commission on the head, & then hurra! for a little out of door work, & excitement, & see if Victoria Crosses can be earned in America as well as India. Lord & myself are the only two officers left here now & most of the men being away the camp looks quite deserted.[15]

Governor Douglas met Captain Snyder at Fort Hope on September 1. He heard the complaints of the Indians, decided liquor was part of the problem and proclaimed the sale or gift of liquor to the Indians to be a penal offence. He received visits from the Thompson River chiefs and "gave them much useful advice for their guidance in the altered state of the country."[16] He also distributed gifts of clothing to the Indian chiefs. Douglas greatly feared an Indian war, for the American miners might appeal to their own government for protection and once the American army moved into the unorganized territory of New Caledonia, it might be difficult to dislodge. However, the discussions between Douglas and the Indian leaders in September 1858, and the presence there of the red-jacketed Royal Engineers, seemed to provide a sense of security. It was obvious that the invasion of the miners could not be stopped and the Indians must salvage what they could, or be exterminated, like many of the Indians south of the border.

In October half the sappers were on the mainland cutting the boundary line from Point Roberts eastwards while the rest were at Esquimalt, assisting with the movement of supplies to the base camps in the Chilliwack valley. Wilson complained that he had to work till five every evening.

Winter has already set in, in the far north, & ducks of numberless varieties, with geese, cranes etc. are arriving in myriads, so numerous indeed that when they are disturbed on the harbour, the flapping of wings can be heard a couple of miles off. I have paid my respects to them once & managed to bag a good many; I can assure you that I look for Saturday afternoon when there is no work as much as ever I did at school.[17]

At this point, Major Hawkins came to announce that Wilson was to take mules and provisions to the Engineer camps near Chilliwack. Aboard the *Otter*, he reached Fort Langley on October 15.

On arriving at Langley I went to see Mr. Yale the chief man there in the H.B.C. & learnt that one of the river steamers would be down next morning. We dined off some very tough beef at the Fort & landed the mules in the pouring rain. The Fort is a miserable old place, built out of pine wood hewed out with axes, & the storehouses surrounded by a rough stockade, with a small bastion, mounting a very old 6 pounder, which I would rather anybody fired off but myself.

When the *Maria* arrived, her engines needed repair. Wilson was impatient to depart, but,

having consulted Mr. Yale on the possibility of getting the mules up the river in bateaux & greatly against our wishes we were obliged to give in to his experience & stay at this dismal place.

COURTESY OF PROVINCIAL ARCHIVES OF BC

Observatory tent, Zenith telescope, of the Boundary Commission, at Yahk River station.

October 21st. I determined to wait no more for the steamer, so having left our muleteer & 4 men with the mules, to come up the river as soon as possible, I got the remainder of the men into a bateau with the baggage & started in pouring rain at 12 o'clock. At 3 we landed to bail out our boat & served some grog round & at 4.45 camped on an island in the middle of the river having made 10 miles, which was good considering the current we had to contend against; we had heavy rain the whole day & night.

October 22nd. Rose at daylight so stiff that I could hardly move; pouring in torrents, & during the night the fall of rain was so great that everything had been saturated, blankets, tents & everything else.... At 3.15 we reached the mouth of the Sumass, nearly 20 miles by my reckoning from where we had spent the night. Shortly after landing the *Maria* hove in sight & I was glad to get the mules safely on shore.

Lieutenant Wilson failed to comment that the two days of rowing in the rain in the open boat could have been avoided if he had taken Mr. Yale's advice. He got back to Esquimalt on October 31 "not at all sorry to get some dry clothes & a roof to sleep under, having been 17 days without a change of clothes & barely 24 hours of fine weather; however neither Lord or myself have felt any ill effects from being so long in wet clothes."

On November 14, he noted that "Some of the Engineers for British Columbia have arrived." The diary reported the arrival at Esquimalt, on December 2, of Mr. Chartres Brew, sent out to organize a provincial police force. Wilson added,

The new judge, Begbie, who has arrived, seems a very good sort of fellow, just the man for a new country. The winter has commenced & occasionally we have had news from the mines; the miners about Thompson's river are in a state of starvation. There is no complaint however about the quantity of gold; it is astonishing what hardships men will undergo for the precious metal. We are quite gay here now, nothing but Balls, private Theatricals, etc.

By Christmas all the sappers were back in their winter quarters in Esquimalt. Wilson wrote of the mud in Victoria as "so deep that it comes up to the horses' girths & foot passengers can only cross on planks laid across."

Last Saturday I made a great expedition to go to a dance. I started in torrents of rain rigged up in long boots & enveloped in a macintosh & rode 8 miles, through the woods, over a most dreadful road, if road it can be called at all, the stumps of the trees in many places still sticking up in the road; I however spent a very pleasant evening for my trouble, but the ride home in the night was dreadful, it rained so hard I could not keep my cigar lighted & had not even that comfort.

The last entry of the year noted that "All the officials for British Columbia have come out here, nearly all Engineer officers; when the *Thames City* arrives we shall have a gathering of the corps." Even as he wrote, the *Thames City* was beating her way south, approaching the Falkland Islands, with the main contingent of the Columbia detachment aboard, fated to enjoy Christmas as best they could on the stormy South Atlantic.

Chapter Two

1858: The Columbia Detachment

On November 14, 1858, just before Wilson returned from his first cold, wet, trip to move the mules to the Sumas prairie, the steamer *La Plata* had arrived from Britain, bringing a small group of Royal Engineers, consisting of Captain Robert Mann Parsons, R.E., and about 20 sappers. This was the first of four parties of Royal Engineers sent out in 1858, and called the "Columbia detachment". The second group, chiefly carpenters, under the command of Captain John Marshall Grant, R.E., followed ten days later, aboard the *Arato* from Panama. The main body of the detachment, under Captain Henry Reynolds Luard, R.E., came around Cape Horn in the *Thames City* and would not arrive until April of the next year. A fourth group, in the ship *Euphrates*, bringing stores, also came by way of the Horn and was a month behind the *Thames City*.

The Engineers' commander, Colonel Richard Clement Moody, R.E., stepped ashore from the *Asia* on Christmas Day, 1858.

When Captain Parsons and his men were ready to depart for North America on September 2, the Secretary of State for the Colonies himself journeyed down to Southampton to wish them well. Sir Edward Bulwer-Lytton, in poor health and growing old, conscious that he was making history, stood on the deck of their ship as she rode the waves off Cowes, and regarded the 21 red-jacketed figures standing stiffly at attention before him, boots polished, pill-box hats at a precise angle. James Duffy was there, fated to freeze to death on a wilderness trail three years later. So was Peter John Leech, who would start a small-scale gold rush of his own in six years. In the line also was John Maclure, whose son, Samuel, would become one of British Columbia's memorable architects. Flags fluttered above them. Lytton had prepared an address, which he read carefully, to control his stutter. He began,

> Soldiers—I have come to say to you a few kind words of parting.
>   You are going to a distant country, not, I trust, to fight against men, but to conquer nature; not to besiege cities, but to create them; not to overthrow kingdoms, but to assist in establishing new communications under the sceptre of your own Queen.
>
>   For these noble objects, you, soldiers of the Royal Engineers, have been especially selected from the ranks of Her Majesty's armies. Wherever you go you carry with you not only English valour and English loyalty, but English intelligence and English skill. Wherever a difficulty is to be encountered which requires in the soldiers not only courage and discipline, but education and science, sappers and miners, the Sovereign of England turns with confidence to you.[1]

When the gold rush struck, Governor Douglas had moved

quickly to impose order and discipline in New Caledonia, where in fact he had neither the authority to do so, nor the military power to enforce his decrees. The British government acted promptly to remedy both these shortcomings. When he had only been in office three weeks as Colonial Secretary, Lytton was prepared to introduce a bill creating the Colony of British Columbia; the bill was read for the first time on July 1, 1858. On July 30 he notified Governor Douglas that he was sending a company of Royal Engineers to British Columbia. He also dispatched administrators, including a judge and a police commissioner. Two new gunboats were especially fitted for service on the northwest coast.

Although the town of Lytton was named after him, the importance of Lytton's contribution to British Columbian history is little known. Handicapped by deafness and a stutter, and dominated by vaulting ambition, Lytton, already a successful novelist and the author of plays and poetry, was determined to make his mark in history as a statesman. The Hudson's Bay officers did not like him, calling him "a visionary Gentleman, who proposed to create some Utopia on the ruins of the Company."[2] Yet he was realistic in his appraisal of the situation in New Caledonia and he wisely chose James Douglas as governor of the new colony as well as the Colony of Vancouver Island, Matthew Begbie as judge and Chartres Brew as police commissioner. He was also responsible for the decision to send, not ordinary soldiers, but the cream of the army, the Royal Engineers. Lytton survived only a short time in office; in the following year when he was gone, the Colonial Office decided that the dispatch of the Royal Engineers had been an error. At Southampton, saying farewell to the first party of Royal Engineers, Lytton continued:

The enterprise before you is indeed glorious. Ages hence industry and commerce will crowd the roads that you will have made; travellers from all nations will halt on the bridges you will have first flung over solitary rivers, and gaze on gardens and cornfields that you will have first

carved from the wilderness; Christian races will dwell in
the cities of which you will map the sites and lay the foundation.[3]

Uncommon soldiers they were and most of them chose to
take their discharge in the new colony and become true pioneers.

Meanwhile, in Victoria, Governor Douglas was coping
with the flood of gold seekers. By 1858, when most of the gold
in California had been found, thousands of idle miners were
searching unsuccessfully for new fields. The gold arriving in
San Francisco in 1857 from the Thompson River was almost
instantly discussed in every saloon in California.

A young Englishman named Kinahan Cornwallis managed
to get aboard the steamer *Cortes* in early June 1858, leaving
San Francisco with nearly 1,500 passengers, bound for Vancouver Island. Observing the American habits of speech and
at table, Cornwallis wrote, "Swarthy, restless fellows, they
walked backwards and forwards and guessed and calculated,
either on deck or in the cabins, from early morning till mid-
night. The same restlessness of tongue and manner
manifested itself during the consumption of their usual meals,
when pork and beans, pickles and molasses, were thrown together on the one plate and hurried into obscurity."[4] On the
morning of the sixth day, the ship arrived at Esquimalt. Cornwallis went ashore with the rest, followed the crowd straight
to the government gold licence office in Victoria where he
paid five dollars for a voucher giving him permission to dig for
a month, and on the afternoon of the same day embarked on
the American steamer *Surprise* "which had just returned from
Fort Hope with Governor Douglas and suite. He is a fine old,
jolly looking Scotchman, very gentlemanly and agreeable."[5]

At Fort Hope Cornwallis joined the miners at the edge of
the river, digging in with the geological shovel he had brought
with him, and in three hours he had $15 in gold. For three
dollars he slept in a tent newly put up by a German, sharing
tea and mutton chops with 14 other miners. After dark, skins

were brought and spread out as beds on the dirt floor, and the residents rolled up in their blankets, their heads resting on their gold. Cornwallis was so excited he could not sleep.

> I did not very readily yield to the embrace of slumber, for the novelty and excitement of my new life kept my thinking powers awake. It was a little past midnight, and the sickly oil lamp which swung from the tent roof still shed its hazy light. Suddenly I heard a rustle and a hissing noise, something between that of a hostler currycombing and stifled laughter. I lifted my head, and directing my eyes towards the tent's opening, beheld a Red Indian, more than six feet in height, holding the canvas drop up, and grinning with evident delight, while the heads and eyes of two or three of his fellows were to be seen peering in the background. "Hillo!" I involuntarily exclaimed. Two or three awoke at the signal and sprang upon their legs as they heard the glee shouts and tramp of the Indians, who bounded off at the instant.[6]

When Cornwallis left Fort Hope to go upriver in June, the spring freshet was already beginning to cover the gravel bars. Through the summer, high water stopped the work on the banks of the Fraser and about 4,000 miners returned to San Francisco in disgust, calling the gold rush the "Fraser River Humbug". However, many, like Cornwallis, inched their way upriver. To avoid the terrifying route through the Fraser Canyon, some miners reached the upper Fraser by following the chain of lakes (Harrison, Seton, Anderson, Lillooet) and connecting streams to Lillooet and then over Pavilion Mountain to the Forks (soon to be named Lytton), a route discovered by Alexander C. Anderson in 1846.

After the stern-wheeler *Umatilla* made a trial run up the Harrison River and Harrison Lake on July 25, Governor Douglas decided to construct a mule trail along this route. Always a practical man, he used the labour immediately available to him: the miners who had been flooded off the bars by

COURTESY OF PROVINCIAL ARCHIVES OF BC

A stern-wheeler at Yale.

the rise of the Fraser River. A crew of 500 was assembled, each man posting a $25 good-behaviour bond and agreeing to work without pay, in return for food and shelter and the privilege of being among the first into the upper Fraser Region, thought to be the location of the "mother lode". The $25 deposit would be repaid in the form of provisions when the road was finished. The work began August 9, at the head of Harrison Lake, where the depot was named Port Douglas in honour of the governor. Completed in October, with 62 wooden bridges, wharfs on the lakes where portages began and ended, and whale-boats for the lakes (contracts being let at the coast for steamers), this mule trail cost the new colony £14,000. Mayne commented, "By this trail the dangers of the passage of the Fraser above Yale are avoided, and a distance of some 120 miles of the most perilous travelling saved. At the worst, when everything had to be carried from one piece of water to the other by Indians, with immense labour and at most extravagant rates of charge, it was far preferable to the river route."[7]

As the river levels dropped at the end of the summer, the miners were able to work the bars once more, and now sluices began to replace rockers and flumes. Possibly 9,000 men were making good wages on the bars. Foreseeing that many of these men would stay through the winter, Douglas ordered the Royal Engineers to lay out the towns of Fort Hope and Fort Yale, and arranged that miners could buy lots on a monthly payment scheme.

Governor Douglas was still at Fort Hope when an interesting visitor arrived. Dr. Carl Friesach, a 37-year-old Austrian mathematics professor, happened to be travelling in North America in 1858 and decided to have a look at this new gold rush. Arriving in Victoria in early September, he got a room at the unfinished Hotel de France and went walking through Victoria. "The houses, with one exception," he remarked, "are built of wood and in such a flimsy manner that a hurricane would certainly carry the whole town away."[8] When he sailed for the Fraser River on the side-wheel steamer *Sea Bird*, the ship caught fire and ran up on a sand bank. Fortunately the smoke attracted the attention of the *Umatilla*, which on July 21 of this same year had been the first steamer to reach Yale, the head of navigation on the Fraser. Professor Friesach slept on the saloon table of the *Umatilla*, covered with coal dust.

Arriving at Fort Hope, a tent city sheltering hundreds of miners, Friesach and his friends introduced themselves to Governor Douglas and accepted his suggestion that they try to reach Fort Yale. They seated themselves in a small boat holding ten people and a large forge bellows. The current was so strong that part of the company was forced to clamber along the rocky edge of the river, towing the canoe by a rope. At the tent city of Fort Yale, they dined in a tent bearing the sign "American Restaurant", sharing the only table and the meal (old fish, dried salmon and undrinkable coffee, which they enjoyed) with "a number of bad characters whom the vigilance committee of San Francisco had sent away".[9] Professor Friesach noted the mixture of people: Americans, Germans, French, Chinese, Italians, Spaniards, Poles, many Indians and only six white women. Crossing the river to visit the famous Hill's Bar, he was "astonished at the enormous amount of gold which was found at Hill's Bar . . . after we had watched the miners for about an hour we returned to Fort Yale, pleased to have seen with our own eyes the wonderful gold mining which was considered by many in San Francisco to be a fable."[10]

The early wave of the gold rush had ebbed by the time Captain Parsons arrived at the end of October with the first group of sappers of the Columbia detachment. These men were immediately taken to Derby, or Old Fort Langley, which Douglas had selected as the capital of the new colony, to begin building the Royal Engineer barracks. The second group of Engineers, under Captain Grant, arriving on November 8, was just eight days ahead of the vessel *Panama*, bringing Matthew Begbie to serve as judge in the new colony. Almost before he had time to unpack, Begbie found himself on his way

COURTESY OF PROVINCIAL ARCHIVES OF BC

Fort Langley. This wood cut appeared in Harper's Weekly *in London, October 9,* 1858.

to Fort Langley, with Governor Douglas and other officials, and with Captain Parsons and his men. The advance parties of sappers had come to the colony just in time to serve as an honour guard at the ceremony proclaiming New Caledonia the Colony of British Columbia.

They all sailed aboard the *Satellite* to Point Roberts and there transferred to the *Otter* and the *Beaver*, the two ships moving slowly up the Fraser River on a sodden, gloomy, November day. When they reached Derby, Captain Parsons and his men disembarked. Surveying their first home in this new land in a downpour of rain, they saw unfinished log buildings and tents awaiting them. There was no time to settle in, for they were to be at the fort nearby on the following morning to add colour to the occasion and to represent the military power of the empire.

At Derby the sappers quickly built log barracks, preparing for the arrival of the main body of the detachment, with all the wives and children, aboard the *Thames City*. However, shortly after their commander, Colonel Moody, arrived in the colony, he vetoed the decision to make Derby the capital, because it was too close to the American border and militarily vulnerable. He chose the site of New Westminster for the capital and Douglas did not contest the decision. Therefore, when the *Thames City* finally arrived, the new camp at the New Westminster site was not ready for them.

With the arrival of Colonel Moody, this amazing year of 1858 drew to a close. The Colony of British Columbia had been created. Governor Douglas had adroitly managed the flood-tide of gold seekers; many of them had gone south to warmer and cheaper places to spend the winter, but some were getting very drunk at Christmas in the log saloons of Fort Hope and Fort Yale. In their unfinished camp at Derby, the newly arrived parties of the Columbia detachment of Royal Engineers celebrated their first Christmas away from home. The Engineers of the Boundary Commission were all back in their winter quarters in Esquimalt, coping with deep mud and dancing until three in the morning. Charles Wilson's entry for December 30 concludes, "I have spent as merry a Christmas as can be expected far away from home; with plenty of work to do there is not much time left to bemoan my fate at being so far away at Xmas."[11]

In many Indian camps there were people dying of starvation, for their preoccupation with the gold rush had interrupted their ancient routines of food gathering for the winter. Many had been earning Yankee dollars and spending the money on bad liquor.

And far away, beating southwards, the *Thames City* failed to reach the Falkland Islands for Christmas. The ship and its passengers were there, however, for New Year's Eve, and when she was a very old lady in Victoria, Mrs. Haynes remembered how the Royal Engineers' band "played the Old Year out and the New Year in, with 'Auld Lang Syne' and the National Anthem. My husband led the music with his clarinet; and while we were all very gay, we couldn't keep back the tears when we thought of the Old England we had left behind, our friends and its Christmas cheer, its roast beef and plum pudding. But when we got to British Columbia, we never regretted coming."[12]

On this same New Year's Eve, in one of the log buildings at Hill's Bar, near Fort Yale, that slippery scoundrel Ned McGowan was sitting amid his cronies in the saloon, plotting some fun to break the monotony of the winter.

Chapter Three

1859: Ned McGowan's "War"

It has been said of Ned McGowan that the only good thing about him was his horse.[1]

Edward McGowan was a man of substance. He had once been a member of the Philadelphia legislature, and was later appointed superintendent of police in that city. When it was discovered that the superintendent had organized a bank robbery, he was forced to leave Philadelphia abruptly to seek wealth in the California gold rush of 1849. On the west coast, his knowledge of law and police administration gained him an appointment as a justice of the peace but again he misused his office, escaping justice by suddenly leaping aboard a ship headed for the Fraser gold rush, where his talents made him the mogul of the Hill's Bar miners' village. In October a report reached Governor Douglas that McGowan "has asserted that Your Excellency had better mind your business in Victoria, for that he was the ruler of Hill's Bar, and that if the miners would only stand by him he would put all Englishmen to defiance and, with words not fit to name, openly declares he will be master of Hill's Bar."[2]

Unable or unwilling to return to California for the winter, Ned had to endure the bitter weather of 1858 at Hill's Bar, where clouds stretched soddenly from mountain to mountain and even the gold-bearing gravel froze. Across the river in Fort Yale presided the self-styled "Captain" P. B. Whannell, justice of the peace, a humourless, egocentric, unbending man. Colonel Moody later described "The bold, insane, reckless zeal, & utter ignorance of Captn Whannell who is incorruptible, full of courage, and despotic as a Czar".[3] On December 29, 1858, Captain Whannell issued a warrant for the arrest of two Hill's Bar men who had assaulted Isaac Dixon of Yale. A message was sent to his colleague at Hill's Bar, asking Justice of the Peace Perrier to arrest the two men. Perrier did so, and sent a man named Hickson to request that Dixon (who was, unaccountably, in jail) be released to appear as witness when the trial was held at Hill's Bar. Whannell, who intended that the matter be tried before him, promptly put Hickson in jail with Dixon. The occupants of the Hill's Bar saloons were outraged. Perrier was persuaded to appoint Ned McGowan as special constable and to write a warrant for the arrest of Captain Whannell for contempt of his (Perrier's) court. Thus authorized, Ned McGowan's gang broke into the Fort Yale jail, released Hickson, secured Dixon, and arrested Whannell who was taken before Perrier and fined $50. When he was free again, Whannell wrote to Governor Douglas, "This town and district are in a state bordering on anarchy; my own and the lives of the citizens are in imminent peril. I beg your Excellency will afford us prompt aid."[4]

Governor Douglas was prompt indeed. Colonel Moody and 25 sappers from Derby under Captain Grant left immediately for Fort Yale, while Captain Prevost set off with 50 marines and seamen aboard the *Plumper*.

In a letter written some weeks after these events, Colonel Moody related that letters had been received from Captain Whannell at Fort Yale

> so alarming and so urgent in their nature that I had no option but instantly to go there & to take the detachment of R.E.'s with me. The Magistrate implored military assistance.... We quickly made our arrangements, hired passages on the only River Steamer, embarked that night & long before daylight we were steaming away up the River. The Men (22 in number) of course delighted, looking up the locks of their Rifles and Revolvers—the Judge & myself grave & thoughtful.... The weather was exceedingly severe, & finally we were all frozen in at a point from whence we could get neither up or down the river.[5]

In this somewhat ridiculous situation, frozen in midstream, Colonel Moody dispatched the Hudson's Bay Company agent

COURTESY OF PROVINCIAL ARCHIVES OF BC

Ned McGowan.

Ogilvy, who happened to be aboard, to reconnoitre the situation at Yale. According to Colonel Moody, Ogilvy went to Hill's Bar:

> Ogilvy, in the dead of the night, walked thro' & among what may be termed the rebel's camp, looked in at the windows of the huts, saw them gambling round the fires, heard their conversations, & was never questioned—the dogs bothered him most—They suspected him. The very night he came back to us a thaw began which enabled us to push on to Fort Hope. I there left the soldiers, determining to go alone up the river to the scene of disturbance, & to quell it all quietly, if it were possible.... Intelligence reached me at Fort Hope that the Governor had sent on the Plumper & some Marines to Fort Langley below in case I might want a reinforcement.... The Judge of course went up with me.[6]

The "intelligence" had been brought to Colonel Moody by a freezing-wet Lieutenant Mayne and a party of ribbon-bedecked Indian paddlers. Mayne had come to Fort Langley aboard the *Plumper* with the marines from Esquimalt. It was decided to hold the reinforcements at Fort Langley and send a message forward to the colonel so Mr. Yale outfitted Mayne and a Mr. Lewis with a canoe and Indian crew and "a blanket, frock and trowsers, a couple of rugs, two or three pipes, plenty of tobacco, tea, coffee, some meat and bread, a frying-pan and saucepan completing my outfit. At this time canoe-travelling was quite new to me."[7] Yale gave him nine stout Indian paddlers dressed in blankets, with large streamers of bright red, blue and yellow ribbons flying from their caps. Yale had given them the ribbons to impress them with the importance of the mission. Mayne's account continued:

> Seating ourselves in the canoe as comfortably as we could, away we started, the frail bark flying over the smooth water, and the crew singing at the top of their wild, shrill voices, their party-coloured decorations streaming in the

bitter winter wind. . . . We paddled along quickly until five o'clock, when we stopped for supper, and, landing, made tea. This meal over, we started again and held on steadily all night. . . . . Indeed, as we swept by a watch-fire near enough for its glare to light up the dark figures straining at their hard work, and their wild swarthy faces, with the long, bright ribbons streaming behind them,—we might well give a shock to some wearied sleeper roused abruptly from dreams of home.[8]

On the second night of Mayne's canoe journey, chunks of ice came hurtling down with the current.

On we pushed, however, and I had fallen asleep when I was suddenly awakened by a sharp crack almost under my head. The canoe had struck a rock in crossing a rapid in the river . . . and she was stove in unmistakeably. The elder of the crew, leaping on to the rock, against which the full force of the current was driving the canoe, lifted her off . . . and the other rowers shooting her ashore, we all jumped out and ran her up upon the snow. Of course everything was wet, ourselves included; but we were too grateful for our narrow escape to heed this trifling inconvenience.[9]

The party of wet men then stumbled the remaining three miles to Fort Hope along a rough path hidden under two or three feet of snow. Mayne's companion Lewis fell once more into the river and was fished out. When they reached Fort Hope they found Colonel Moody, Captain Grant and Judge Begbie gathered around the fire in Mr. Ogilvy's room at the Hudson's Bay fort. Mr. Ogilvy gave them dry clothes and a hot supper. The next morning, in brilliant sunlight, Moody, Begbie, Lieutenant Mayne and a small party went on up the river to Fort Yale in a small boat, stopping to chat with the miners on the bars. As Colonel Moody had only arrived in British Columbia a few weeks earlier, this was his first examination of the Fraser. He wrote,

The scenery was very grand all the way, & as "Bar" succeeded "Bar" with Miners all at their work at their
"Rockers" and Sluices gathering in the Gold dust, it had a
very lively cheerful look. The blue smoke from their log
cabins curled up among the trees.... The trees being
chiefly Cedar and Black Spruce contrasted with the daz-
zling Snow. The river was alternately "Rapids" and "Still-
water" reflecting every thing—Reflecting cottages, blue
smoke, trees, mountains & moving figures. A scene full of
life. The sun shone splendidly over all.... My heart was
overflowing with earnest love for all these manly energetic
fellows.[10]

The crowd awaiting his arrival at Yale included the
notorious Ned McGowan.

They gave me a Salute, firing off their loaded Revolvers
over my head—Pleasant—Balls whistling over one's head!
as a compliment! Suppose a hand had dropped by accident!
If it was to try my nerves they must have forgotten my pro-
fession. I stood up, & raised my cap & thanked them in the
Queen's name for their loyal reception of me—It struck the
right chord, & I was answered by 3 long loud cheers—I
passed down their ranks, saying something friendly right &
left.

The day after my arrival at Fort Yale was a Sunday & I sent
round to invite everybody to meet me at Divine Service in
the Court House—It was the 1st time in B. Columbia that
the liturgy of our Church was read.... The room was
crowded full of Hill's Bar men as well as others, old grey
bearded men, young eager eyed men, stern middle aged
men, of all nations, knelt with me before the throne of
Grace.

At that moment it seemed as if the whole affair had dis-
sipated, like the blue smoke from the miners' huts. However,

Miners at a way-side house. Taken from Cheadle's book of his travels in
1862.

Governor Douglas had ordered Colonel Moody to dismiss
Perrier, the Hill's Bar justice of the peace. The next day,
when this was done, the Hill's Bar crowd was incensed.
Colonel Moody stated that

> Ned McGowan in great excitement struck a ruler of the op-
> posite party in the face [Dr. Fifer]—many persons were in
> evident terror, & one gentleman who desired to bring me
> information sent me word that he was besieged in his
> house. . . . It was necessary to bring up the detachment of
> R.E.'s fr Fort Hope & I was most anxious that not even a
> spark shd get alight, that all shd be at once crushed, and an
> example be shown as to what we cd do. I ordered up to Fort
> Hope the marines (30) fr Langley & some Seamen with 2
> Field Pieces—I despatched Lt. Mayne R.N. with 2 Indians
> in a light canoe—They started in the dark & pulled hard—
> The R.E.'s had gone to bed when he arrived—In an hour
> they were up & on the water under Captn Grant—By

Mayne I had sent very careful written instructions to Grant as to his movements.

From Fort Hope, while Lieutenant Mayne and his Indians went on downriver to bring up the reinforcements, Captain Grant and the sappers started up the river to Fort Yale, having sent Ogilvy ahead in a small canoe to listen along the river bank and discover if the Hill's Bar men were preparing an ambush. Grant and the sappers followed him, disembarking just below Hill's Bar, on the opposite side of the river. According to Colonel Moody's account,

At Break of day the Hill's Bar Men saw the detachment filing past between the trees on the opposite bank & they ran down shouting & firing off their rifles. It might have been & probably was only a bravado. Grant says he heard no bullets, but . . . they just marched steadily on but with a look of a very determined character, while on the opposite side of the River all was shouting & excitement. I walked down to meet them after their bitterly cold night's march. Ogilvy & Macdonald in the advance & quite in their element, you saw "enjoyment" on their faces—With respect to my own good fellows I have only to say they are "Royal Engineers" that is surely enough. . . . Fr the moment of their arrival everything began to change & to brighten up. Alarm vanished & Hill's Bar Men were full of assurances to everybody that they were & always had been loyal men, & that to say otherwise was to libel them.

The arrival of the Royal Engineers at Fort Yale in January of 1859 was the turning point. The next day a trial was held concerning Ned McGowan's jail-breaking, assault on Whannell and attack on Dr. Fifer. "After the Sappers came, one constable was quite sufficient to execute the summons anywhere, not I believe fr fear exactly, but because their eyes were opened for the first time to see that in the Queen's dominions an infringement of the Law was really a serious matter, & not a sort of half joke as in California", Moody re-marked. For the first two offences, McGowan gained dis-missal on the grounds that he had been appointed a special constable. Colonel Moody's letter gives Ned McGowan much praise for the conduct of his own defence:

> The trial came off in the Court House—it was very crowd-ed—the miners armed to the teeth—McGowan armed—the only unarmed men were the Judge & myself—I wd not even have my "Orderly", & the Sappers were removed to the further end of the Town. Ned McGowan pleaded guilty, & made an exquisitely beautiful speech, so neat, such few words, all to the point, nothing discursive, no "bunkism", no nonsense of any kind, admirable for what he left out as well as for what he said—It was in fact a very clever & very gentlemanly speech—dignified and yet respectful—Begbie inflicted the greatest fine he cd & caused him to enter into recognizances to keep the peace—He also delivered a very manly address what you might expect fr an Englishman who has a high courage—He gave it to McGowan very heavily, & stripped bare all their false definitions of right & wrong. The fine was paid down at once & recognizances entered into, and all was at an end.

Emerging from the courthouse, Judge Begbie and Lieutenant Mayne accepted an invitation to visit Hill's Bar. Ned McGowan himself conducted them over the diggings and then "invited us to a collation in his hut where we drank champagne with some twelve or fifteen of his California min-ing friends. . . . I have rarely lunched with a better-spoken, pleasanter party."[11] The day after the trial, Moody suddenly collapsed. He blamed his sudden fainting on

> the excessive cold, the daily wet feet, cold up to my knees in snow & sludge, sleeping on all manner of things. All the time I was at Yale, I slept on three boxes in a passage! (My

Orderly & the Judge side by side on the floor) very bad in-
digestible food etc. etc. and not a little pressure of thought
on my brain, all combined to upset me at the last—the
whole party Judge & Soldiers had had cholic & diarrhea
more or less from the continued exposure, bad living with
constant cold & wet & I had escaped hitherto. I suppose
"Mind" had kept my body going but when all was quiet I
broke down—almost fainted.[12]

Now the reinforcements and Chartres Brew with the constables arrived, adding to the display of force. For a colony
only two months old, with few sources of income, it had been
an expensive but effective show of power. Ludicrous as the incident may seem, this comic opera "war" set the pattern for a
well-regulated and non-violent gold rush and the peaceful development of the new colony. As for Ned McGowan, he soon
left for California with $4,700 in gold in his poke. The time
had come for him to sell his horse and depart.

Chapter Four

1858–1859: The *Thames City*

In his book of 1862, Lieutenant Mayne wrote of the length of the voyage around the southern tip of South America. "The drawback to this [route] is the length of the sea-voyage, which may be said to average five months, although it has been done in four."[1] The *Thames City* took six. The *Thames City* was a clipper-built ship, three-masted and square-rigged. She had left Gravesend on October 10, 1858. On board, besides Captain Glover and the ship's crew, were Captain Luard, Lieutenants Lemprière and Palmer, the surgeon J. V. Seddall, 118 non-commissioned officers and sappers, 31 women and 34 children.

A week or so after the departure from Gravesend, the entire company gathered on the deck for the reading of the first edition of a newspaper, *The Emigrant Soldier's Gazette and Cape*

Horn Chronicle, hand-written in the neat script of Second Corporal Charles Sinnett, who was also the editor. His assistant was Lieutenant Palmer. Everyone was dressed in their best, because the reading of the newspaper, with music and dancing to follow, was an important social occasion. The ship moved sedately across the Bay of Biscay, the great sails above full of wind, the sea heaving gently. Captain Luard began to read:

> We have started on a long voyage for a distant land with no prospect for several months of any fresh faces to be seen, or any fresh beef to be eaten. . . . [2]

The editor reprinted a leading article from *The Times* of London which stated that

COURTESY OF PROVINCIAL ARCHIVES OF BC

Captain Henry Reynolds Luard, RE.

Whenever Her Majesty's Government want a body of skilful, intelligent and industrious mechanics to perform any
task requiring peculiar judgment, energy and accuracy,
such as ... the construction of houses, roads and bridges,
in a new Colony, they have only to turn to the Corps of
the Royal Engineers and they find all the material they
want.[3]

Not only were they skilful, intelligent and industrious, but
they could also claim musical talent. Sapper William Haynes
could play almost any woodwind or brass instrument, and on
the passage to British Columbia he taught himself to play the
violin. In fact Captain Glover was finally forced to order him
aloft: "Haynes, you can take the squeaky fiddle up to the rigging and make all the hell you want to up there, but you can't
do it on deck!"[4] There were at least 12 musicians in the sapper
band, and Captain Luard and Staff-Assistant Surgeon Seddall
played fine duets on flute and harmonium. After the reading
of the current issue of the ship's newspaper, the company of
the *Thames City* danced on the deck in the darkening evening
to the melodies of the sapper musicians.

These were happy times, before the heat of the tropics became oppressive and the band stopped practising in the after-
noons. Mrs. Haynes remembered that "in such crowded
quarters, we took the hoops out of our gowns."[5] The married
couples had little privacy in that area of bunks called "The
Dovecote", which did not always have the aura of cooing
serenity the name suggests. Some time during November, the
wife of Acting Quarter Master Sergeant D. S. Osment gave
birth to a daughter, in the awkward circumstances of a bunk
in the Dovecote. On November 24, John Linn's son and heir
was born. The infant's mother, Mary Linn, lived to have five
children more and to help establish a pioneer farm at Lynn
Creek, North Vancouver. On November 25 a sombre company gathered on the deck to sing hymns and pray, before the
body of little Richard Bridgeman, son of Sergeant Richard
Bridgeman, slid into the swaying sea. Everyone was greatly

relieved when, five days after the death of her son Richard, Mrs. Bridgeman successfully gave birth to a daughter.

"What we missed most were vegetables and fruit," Mrs. Haynes recalled. Dr. Seddall insisted that everyone drink lime juice. The ship carried "cows, so our children could have milk; sheep to start a flock when we got to the new colony; chickens for our breakfast eggs—and not too many, at that; and a rooster that crowed at dawn."[6] Cows, pigs, sheep, chickens and a goat (which produced twin kids during the voyage) were kept in the hold in the area called Long-Boat Square, where the men had to take turns with the shovel.

As the *Thames City* crossed the equator, King Neptune with a cardboard crown and a three-pronged pitchfork climbed over the rail, dripping sea water. The tribute required was the hair on the chins of the uninitiated. The lather for shaving was "manufactured from marine soap, tar, a few trifling collections from the sheep pen and other maritime perfumes."[7] There was one man for whom the initiation was especially painful, and his anguish was witnessed by two small boys, John Henry Scales, the son of Sapper John Scales, and John McMurphy, the son of Sergeant-Major John McMurphy. When these boys were old men in their nineties, they still recalled the frustrated misery of the doctor, John Vernon Seddall, when he lost his beautiful beard. Eighty-seven years later a headline in the *Province* would read: "Shaved and shorn, Dr. Seddall wept."[8] Seddall, a quiet reserved man, was proud indeed of a fine silky beard reaching almost to his waist, dark brown with a red tint. When it was smeared with tar, pitch and dirt, there was nothing to do but shave it off and Seddall wept tears of outrage.

A different kind of entertainment was provided by the "Theatre Royale", which offered plays. "A Thumping Legacy" featured "Miss Matilda" (played by Henry Hazel, whose feelings were later hurt by a joking remark in the *Gazette* and who then refused to play the feminine leads). The Theatre Royale, managed by Corporal Alfred Howse, produced "Bombastes Furioso", "She Stoops to Conquer" and

COURTESY OF PROVINCIAL ARCHIVES OF BC

Staff-Assistant Surgeon John Seddall, RE.

"Cool as a Cucumber". The officers contributed one evening's entertainment when Captain Luard, Lieutenant Palmer and Dr. Seddall performed "Box and Cox", with Dr. Seddall (without beard) playing Mrs. Bouncer. Once, when a play had to be postponed because one of the actors was ill, the company listened to Captain Luard read Charles Dickens' *Poor Traveller.* Some of the sappers formed a group of Christy's Minstrels, singing "Oh, Susanna, don't you cry for me" and "Carry me back to Old Virginny."

They had hoped to reach the Falklands by Christmas, but contrary winds forced them to celebrate the holiday on the high seas with "pork in place of turkey, plum pudding, extra grog, a snapdragon for the children and a dance for all."[9] (A snapdragon is a rum-soaked, flaming mixture of raisins, dates, nuts and candy.) The Royal Engineers anticipated a warm welcome at Port William, Stanley Harbour, because their Commander, Colonel Moody, had for nine years been Governor of the Falkland Islands. They were not disappointed. "It was grand to eat English roast beef and Yorkshire pudding after the long, weary diet of bully beef and hard tack,"[10] Mrs. Haynes remembered. Sapper Thomas Gilchrist's son was born, Thomas Price had a daughter, and Fanny and Jonathan Morey's daughter also arrived, appropriately named Marina. The *Thames City* passengers helped prepare for the island wedding of Mr. Huthlicaut and his bride and everyone enjoyed the feast.

After New Year's Eve, when the band "played the Old Year out and the New Year in", it was time to continue their voyage. The *Thames City* had passed through the Straits of Magellan when the worst of the storms hit her. The passengers got into their bunks, some having to be lashed in. Suddenly there was a tremendous crash and a ripping, rending noise. Some screamed, and everyone thought that the ship had hit something. In terror they waited for the icy water to come flooding in. Then there was the sound of a heavy chain rattling, and they realized that the anchor chain had broken away. Men rushed to the hold and got the chain boxed before it could do any damage. Mrs. Haynes admitted, "I can tell you there were times when we were all badly scared."[11]

The storm gradually subsided, but the weather was grey and depressing. Sapper George Newton's wife died and was buried at sea. They stopped at Valparaiso but were not allowed ashore. Mrs. Haynes recalled the bumboat women:

Captain Glover was a wise old bird. He had more sense than let his sailormen off the ship at Valparaiso. He had no mind to lose any of them to those giddy senoritas. There were big, bold, bumboat women too, with curtain rings in their ears and gay colored head-dresses, who were allowed to come on board to sell us things. They came out to our ship with fruit and curios, in little cockleshell boats.[12]

Riding the tide out of Valparaiso harbour, the *Thames City* headed north again. They made about 115 miles each day, or about 4¾ miles each hour. In early February the sun emerged from the clouds, "warming the laughing faces of the children who came swarming up like butterflies on a summer day, from the recesses of the between decks."[13] However, as they re-entered the tropics, the heat became oppressive and the editor of the *Gazette* admitted, "Well, it is precious hot, there's no doubt of it. Even the children are bad tempered. Or perhaps... everyone is tired of this horrid long voyage."[14]

At last the Flattery Rocks were sighted and the ship rode into the Strait of Juan de Fuca. Pushed by a westerly breeze, the vessel soon reached Race Rocks where the swift outrush of the tide of the Strait of Georgia swung the prow a few degrees. As the ship entered Esquimalt Harbour, the sails were clewed up. Slowly the ship came up to Jones's landing-place. The *Thames City* had arrived at last.

Mrs. Haynes, when she was 82 and a little old lady with pink cheeks, blue eyes and silvery hair, still remembered that moment of bursting joy. "The men of the first two bodies of Royal Engineers, who had preceded us some time before, were on the dock to greet us and to accompany us to the Hudson's Bay wharf in Victoria. My! how daft they were with delight, to see their women and children again! and they gave us a grand ball, at which we danced and were happy until dawn!"[15]

Chapter Five

1859: "The Labours of the Engineers"

"After we had got our belongings straightened out, after the joy of welcome had subsided, we were put on board the *Eliza Anderson*, commanded by Capt. John Irvine, and sent up the Fraser to the point of debarkation. There were no wharves at New Westminster. There was no town. We had to go ashore in little boats,"[1] explained Mrs. Haynes. Although some of the sappers went to New Westminster to build the accommodations for the Royal Engineers, most of the *Thames City* passengers were taken to the completed buildings at Derby, and were transferred to New Westminster some months later. They took with them to Derby one of the biggest bakings Victoria had ever done—2,000 loaves—to be consumed during the chaotic days of getting settled in their temporary home.

This was not the way Governor Douglas had planned their reception. When he had chosen Derby to be the capital he had forestalled speculators by declaring all lands there to be Crown property. Following Douglas's orders, J. D. Pemberton held a public auction of building lots in Derby, collecting over $66,000 for the treasury. Fearing that the sale of lots at Derby and the work done by the advance parties of sappers would influence the British government to choose that site as the capital, Colonel Moody argued that the lots could be exchanged for others at Queenborough (New Westminster), that at Derby "scarcely any buildings of consequence are up, except a building intended to receive some of my men", and that the site couldn't be defended. "At any moment the Americans could and would have their grip on the very throat of British Columbia."[2]

Returning from Ned McGowan's "War" in January, Lieutenant Mayne had examined the site Colonel Moody had chosen for the capital. He thought it good, from a strategic point of view,

> but the bush there was very thick. Dr. Campbell and I went to examine a part a little north of where the town stands, and so thick was the bush that it took us two hours to force our way in rather less than a mile and a half. Where we penetrated, it was composed of very thick willow and alder, intertwined so closely that every step of the way had to be broken through, while the ground was cumbered with fallen timber of a larger growth. During this scramble I stumbled upon a large bear, which seemed to be as much surprised to see me as I was at sight of him, and I dare say equally discomposed.[3]

On February 1 Colonel Moody waited impatiently for the Colonial Office to decide whether Derby or Queenborough would be the capital. "Among other extreme inconveniences caused by the delay will be extra cost when the "Thames City" arrives. I ought now to be preparing for their reception

& I don't know what to do. If Queenborough is to be the place
then the site for the Barracks & Engineer Stores must be in
the neighborhood. It is very perplexing."[4] Two weeks later,
the decision arrived from London: Queenborough was the
capital of the new colony. Not until summer was the name of
the city settled; on July 20, 1859, Governor Douglas announced Queen Victoria's decision: it would be called New
Westminster, not Queenborough.

Colonel Moody immediately ordered sappers to the new
site. Arthur Thomas Bushby, a charming young man who fell
in love with Governor Douglas's daughter, Agnes, and who
was made a clerk of the courts by Judge Begbie, visited
Queenborough on March 12, 1859, three weeks after
Douglas's proclamation, and found that "as yet there are only
two wooden huts there, one for Col. Moody & the other for
the men—what a glorious sight the downright wooden log
hut, a fireplace big enough to roast an ox & such a fire—logs
too big for me to lift. We had a regular pic-nic lunch. . . .
Queenborough is a beautiful site—and the life there as yet is
savage and jovial in the vengeance."[5] On April 10, two days
before the arrival of the *Thames City*, the *Plumper*, with
Lieutenant Mayne aboard, took 20 sappers to Queenborough
"which place had since our last visit become the head-quarters
of what military force was stationed in British Columbia."[6]

A complaint recorded from this period is in the handwriting of the colonel's lady, Mary Moody, waiting, with her four
children, in Victoria until a house had been built at Queenborough. In a letter to her mother, she confessed, "I used to
have a good cry every time your letters came, but Richard did
not approve of my crying every fortnight, so I have had to
give it up."[7]

Colonel Moody also complained. Arthur Blackwood of the
Colonial Office was told in a letter dated February 1, 1859,
that Colonel Moody wrote "amidst 10,000 distractions, &
snatched at the intervals of business. . . . Never do I believe
did a man "work" under greater disadvantages than I am now

doing. . . . No Office, no Clerks, a very tiny house full of my dear Children but whose shouts sometimes "fun" sometimes "wailing" do not tend to compose the thoughts."[8] By Easter Mrs. Moody was able to describe to her sister the accommodations awaiting her in Queenborough: "Our own house will not be ready for some weeks but we are to have a 4 roomed house wh. has been put up for us by Capn. Parsons, and we are to have a tent for a drawing room! I think it will be most charming."[9] After moving to Queenborough on May 18 aboard the *Beaver*, she wrote, "I know nobody who does not regret having come out here. Many return by the next boat. Had I been in travelling condition I am sure Richard would have left by the next steamer after Christmas—at least he says so."[10] Nothing in the records supports this contention, but no doubt the reality of the New World was much harsher than anticipated.

The Reverend John Sheepshanks, appointed temporary chaplain to the Engineers, arrived at Queenborough in mid-summer of 1859:

On turning a corner of the river, after an hour or two of steady steaming up stream, at about fifteen miles from the mouth of the river, the captain, who was standing by my side, said, 'There, sir, that is your place.' I looked up a long stretch of the river and there on the left hand side I saw a bit of a clearing in the dense forest. Mighty trees were lying about in confusion, as though a giant with one sweep of his mighty arm had mown them down. Many of the trunks had been consumed by fire. Their charred remains were seen here and there. The huge stumps of the trees were still standing in most places . . . and between the prostrate trees and stumps there were a few huts, one small collection of wooden stores, some sheds and tents, giving signs of a population of perhaps 250 people. This clearing continued up river to the extent of somewhat more than a quarter of a mile . . . this was New Westminster.[11]

New Westminster, about 1863.

Lieutenant Mayne explained,

> There is no fault to be found with New Westminster; but
> the forest is so dense, and the trees of which it is composed
> so large, that its growth is likely for some years to be very
> slow. Indeed, had it not been for Colonel Moody's
> determination to make a beginning, and for the labours of
> the Engineers in clearing the site of their camp, New West-
> minster would have made little, if any, perceptible pro-
> gress.... Of the severity of that labour, no one unac-
> quainted with the difficulty of clearing bush as it exists in
> British Columbia can form any accurate concept."[12]

Governor Douglas was concerned not only with the high
expenses relating to clearing and surveying the new capital
but with the fact that the work of building their camp and
clearing the site of Queenborough prevented the Royal
Engineers from getting at the essential work of road construction. Moreover, Colonel Moody's plans for parks and avenues
at New Westminster seemed extravagant to the governor,

who was more keenly aware of the poverty of the colonial treasury. It was only with difficulty that the governor was able to get some accounting of expenditures from Captain William Driscoll Gosset, a friend of Colonel Moody's, who had been sent by the Colonial Office to serve as treasurer of the colony. The early accord between Douglas and Moody did not survive the wrangling over money. However, stores, churches and houses were being built amid the stumps, and the outraged purchasers of lots at Derby were allowed to transfer the cost towards payment for lots at New Westminster.

In temporary accommodation in the new city, on June 1, 1859, Mrs. Moody wrote to her sister, Emily Hawks, that

Camping is very pleasant when the sun shines, but we looked most pitiable in the wet! Our kitchen is off the house, so that we are not annoyed with the heat of the Stove in the small rooms. Mr. Nichol has just come in fr. Port Douglas, so he & Richard are chatting away at a tremendous rate. . . . Thank you dear Em very much for sending the socks, they will be most acceptable as you wd. also think if you saw the state of the white cotton ones in this *dusty* place—We are really most comfortably "fixed" here— The House does very nicely for Summer, and the Govt. has granted [undecipherable] for our house . . . the site staked out, and the Contractor now making his estimate & promises to have it "up" in 2 or 3 months, so by the time this reaches you, you may begin to fancy us expanding into dining room, drawing-room, kitchen & pantry etc. etc. *Now* we have 3 visitors, Mrs. Cochrane & her Baby—Mr. Nichol, & Mr. Langford—So you see these "balloon" houses as these "run-up" wooden ones are called, are also expansive—Mrs. Cochrane is here for her husband is gone down to Victoria, and she was to be left at Queenborough in a Tent alone, surrounded with workmen etc. so I told her to come up to our spare Tent, however the rain came on, & I cd. not let her go into the wet damp tent with her Baby, so she has Dick's bed, Dick Kitty's in the Nursery, she on the floor, Mr. Langford the spare tent—Capn. Nichol my bed in Richd's tent, me on the Sofa in the Sitting room. I was obliged to give in to this as *I* have to pass thro' the Sitting room to the Tent in dressing Gown, and if Mrs. Cochrane wanted anything during the night she has to come into the Sitting room—So you see a man wd. be 'de trop'.

At the end of the letter, Mrs. Moody gave her family further glimpses of life in the new settlement:

Quite a sensation the arrival of the Boat, & discovering what the Butcher has sent for us all—Sometimes he treats one better than another, & then we "go shares"—The Dr.

Mary Susannah Moody.

COURTESY OF PROVINCIAL ARCHIVES OF BC

Colonel Richard Clement Moody, RE.

[Seddall] "caters" for the Mess so when he hears of any-thing good he tells me & so I do to him. The Garden gets on wonderfully. We have splendid radishes now wh. are a great treat—I send you a photograph of the Garden, the man sitting down wh. the watering pots is Haines [Sapper William Haynes, Bandmaster], the Sapper gardener. The house is the Gardener's—I do not think I have anything else to tell you excepting that it is *very, very* hot. I dislike hot weather very much—and it has a very bad effect on the Children's tempers![13]

"Chatting away at a tremendous rate" Captain Nichol dis-cussed with Colonel Moody the latest reports from the Royal Engineers working on the Harrison-Lillooet road to the gold-fields. The mule route built by the 500 miners the previous year was in operation, but costs were high. The Royal Engineers were given the task of making a broad wagon road to replace the narrow mule trail between Port Douglas and Lillooet Lake and from Pemberton to Anderson Lake. Sergeant-Major John McMurphy was there: "I left New Westminster June 1859 with a detachment of Engineers for Douglas, made a trail there to 10-mile House."[14]

One of the main engineering difficulties was at the very beginning of the route: the Harrison River was "in one spot so shallow, that the steamers, when the water is low, have to land their cargoes on the bank, and boats inside the bar reship them for Port Douglas."[15] According to Lieutenant Mayne, it was "decided to make a canal through the flat, deepening it and walling it up with large baulks of timber. This task gave Captain Grant and a party of 80 sappers very moist occupation for two summers, and still I believe baffles their labours."[16] The sappers put in a series of pilings at a certain angle, with logs connecting pairs of pilings to form baulks, underwater barriers against which the current swept, so the river was forced to scour its own channel. It was an ingenious solution and it apparently worked. Lieutenant Mayne may have written his comments before the success of the installations had been demonstrated.

Three sappers, James H. Elliott, William Manstrie and Edward H. Roe, died during the work. *The Colonist* of March 24, 1860, reported that:

> The *Otter* arrived about five o'clock last evening from New Westminster. W. T. Balou Esq. of the Express sends on the Particulars of the drowning of three members of the Sappers and Miners' Corps, recently sent up to improve the Harrison River Rapids, while attempting to return in a canoe to the camp from the mouth of the river on Saturday evening last. On making a crossing about half a mile below the camp (a terrible gale blowing at the time) the boat capsized and three out of the four occupants were hurried into eternity.[17]

It was while he was working out of Port Douglas that young Robert Butler, the Engineers' bugler, helped capture a murderer. An Indian, hired as a packer by the miners, had killed his employers for the gold they carried. The Indian, and a French miner with 50 pounds of gold wrapped in a blanket, paused to drink from a brook beside the Douglas trail, and while the miner was bending to scoop up the water, the Indian shot him, but the bullet only grazed his shoulder. At this moment, Robert Butler and two other sappers came along the trail. The Indian darted into the forest, the sappers in pursuit. Agile, 17-year-old Butler was able to catch the fugitive, who, at his trial, was shown to have killed at least eight men.

While some of the Royal Engineers were widening the mule trail to Lillooet and others were building the baulks in the Harrison River, Colonel Moody ordered a survey of the North Road to Burrard Inlet, so that New Westminster would have an alternate route for supplies or military reinforcements, if such should be required. According to R. C. Harris, the standard road width was one chain (66 feet or 20 metres) but early road contractors were required to clear an aisle only three to six metres wide. The Royal Engineers drew up the plans and specifications for the road, received tenders for its construction, and later supervised and accepted the completed work. The trail from the camp to Burrard Inlet, laid out and cut through in 1859, had a steep descent at the north end. The 1859 trail was widened to a wagon road in 1861. North Road still runs straight as a ruler north from New Westminster, widening to six traffic lanes at the Lougheed Mall.

The report in *The Colonist*, Victoria's newspaper, of the first celebration of Queen Victoria's birthday in New Westminster (still called Queenborough) described the sports and games, the "large concourse of people", the parading of the troops (Royal Engineers as well as marines from the *Plumper*) and their inspection by Colonel Moody, the *Plumper* decorated with flags, the enthusiastic cheering for Colonel Moody and his wife, the wives and children entertained with tea and cake provided by Mrs. Moody, and the music of a band composed of musicians from the Royal Engineers and from the *Plumper*. The reporter remarked that "Queenborough is by no means the 'slough of despond' that some persons are prone to promulgate". Following the account of the festivities a separate item informed the readers that "Lieut. Gov. Moody and lady cheered by the people at Queenborough. Gov. Douglas, without his lady, at Beacon Hill races, Victoria, almost unnoticed."[18]

Away from the jollity at Queenborough, by May 1859 nearly all the Royal Engineers of the Boundary Commission were working in the Cascades. A meeting was held at Semiahmoo Bay with the American Commission; Charles Wilson recorded little of the meeting, but his remarks give a glimpse of the Strait of Georgia islands in their primordial glory:

> I cannot describe to you the scenery of the islands, as it baffles all description ... it was like walking through a flower bed in an English garden, the flowers were nearly all new to me & some of them very beautiful & would be prized in any English garden. I collected a great many & pressed them as well as I could.[19]

At first the boundary survey work went well.

> June 10 (Chilukweyuk [Chilliwack] depot). I am here with 15 men, erecting a depot store from which our supplies can be pushed right into the mountains. We are in for hard work & no mistake this summer. At present I have only been here about 5 days & have been working hard all the time clearing away the thick bush & building a shanty. The scenery is most lovely but as far as I have seen the place abounds in snakes, mosquitoes, sand flies, rain & thunder with an occasional roasting day up to 113; the night air comes down excessively cold from the mountains so that we generally turn into the blankets early. I am at present

seated on a powder barrel & scribbling away with my case on my knees.... Mosquitoes very vicious this evening & drive their stings right through my cord trousers, but I feel, as Mark Tapley would say, 'excessively jolly' & think I ought to have been a backwoodsman all my life.

The mosquitoes soon dampened Wilson's enthusiasm. This plague is, for the most part, a thing of the past, as is the wild and lovely wilderness which produced it:

June 16 (Headquarters Camp, Chilukweyuk Prairie). My office marquee is now set up, but the mosquitoes are something fearful.... We have in camp here present, the Commissioner, Lyall, Lord & myself.... I think this is the most beautiful place I was ever in, the prairie though small in comparison to the ones on the other side of the mountains, is most lovely, covered with flowers & strawberries & even in this early period of the year the grass is nearly up to the waist.

June 19th. Roche's return mule train came in from a mountain gorge called Tommeahai this evening & I am sorry to say the news are rather bad, one mule had fallen over a precipice & broken its neck, the burthen all lost & one man broken his leg, a compound fracture it is believed; poor fellow he will have to lie in the woods till Lyall can get up to him; so you see we are beginning to experience a little roughing. My present dress consists of a very bad jim crow, a red serge shirt with pockets, a blue serge pair of trousers, stockings & mocassins, a huge gauze bag over my head & a short pipe puffing vigorously to try & keep the 'squitoes' off.

July 27th. I must not pass over this day without mentioning the kindness of an Indian chief & his family who were fishing near our halt. I had arrived some time before the train & having tied my horse went to have a chat with them; the old chief's wife took compassion on my wretched state [due to mosquitoes] & having asked my permission, they brought out the paint bag & painted my face & hands with vermilion & certainly the relief was very great; you would have laughed to have seen me painted up like an Indian; after the operation a pipe was lighted & passed round the circle, everybody, women included, taking 3 or 4 puffs. . . . My hands, during the last few days, have been so swollen & stiff that I could hardly bend my joints & have had to wrap them in wet towels to be ready for the next day's work. Two of Darrah's mules have been blinded & 6 of our horses were so reduced that we had to turn them out on the prairie & let them take their chance of living. I never saw anything like the state of their skins, one mass of sores.

COURTESY OF PROVINCIAL ARCHIVES OF BC

Lieutenant Charles Wilson, RE.

During this summer of 1859, while the Royal Engineers of the Boundary Commission contended with mosquitoes, gold was discovered on the Similkameen River to the east, and then at Rock Creek, very close to the 49th parallel. Immediately, Lieutenant Palmer was sent to survey a route from Hope into the new gold area, so that trade would not go south. For this task his equipment was probably much the same as the gear Lieutenant Mayne described for a running survey of the Fraser River in the same summer. His corduroy trousers were tied under the knee "to take the drag off it when they are wet." He carried an aneroid and a spy-glass over his shoulder and a chronometer in his pocket. For food he had a side or two of bacon, four or five bags of flour, plenty of tea and coffee, and a bottle of brandy for emergencies. "Our fare upon occasions like this consisted almost exclusively of bacon and dampers, with tea and coffee. Now and then we might be lucky enough to shoot a grouse." Dampers were "cakes of dough rolled out to the size of a plate, and one or two inches thick. They are cooked either by being baked in the wood-ashes of the fire, or fried in the pan with bacon fat." It was also necessary to take a sextant and artificial horizon for determining latitude and longitude. To carry the gear, he required nine Indians at two dollars a day "which, with their food, was the lowest price at which the Indians would work",[20] each Indian carrying 50 or 60 pounds.

Lieutenant Palmer went east from Fort Hope as far as Fort Colville, the most northerly Hudson's Bay fort in Washington territory. With him, as far as the present village of Tulameen, was Judge Begbie with a small retinue, *en route* to Kamloops on judicial duties. Palmer's report recorded the sight of the bones of 60 or 70 Hudson's Bay fur brigade horses, which had not survived a difficult trip over Manson's Mountain a few years earlier.

Also in the summer of 1859, Lieutenant A. R. Lemprière and a small party of sappers were cutting a trail from Hope up the Coquihalla River for six miles, then up Boston Bar Creek, over a mountain ridge and along the Anderson River which flows northward to join the Fraser River at Boston Bar. This mule trail bypassed some of the most dangerous parts of the Fraser Canyon but the high pass (4,500 feet) to the Anderson River was closed by snow for weeks longer than the trails at lower altitudes. Also, it was a very long, tortuous route, subject to landslides. The mileage on the various routes up the Fraser was as follows:

1848 Old Mountain Trail, Yale to Boston Bar ...34 miles
1859 Boston Bar Trail, via Coquihalla,
         Hope to Boston Bar .... 60 miles
1863 Cariboo wagon road, Yale to Boston Bar ..25 miles[21]

Suddenly, everyone talked about San Juan Island and war. The Oregon Treaty of 1846 stated that when the 49th parallel reached the western sea it was to pass through "the channel" which separated the continent from Vancouver Island. Unfortunately there are several islands and three possible channels: Rosario Strait (next to the Washington coast), Middle Channel (bisecting what are now called the San Juan Islands), and Haro Strait (along Vancouver Island). Neither the British nor the Americans were willing to give up their claims to the cluster of islands, so the dispute had been referred by the two sets of Boundary Commissioners to their respective governments. However, before any decision had been made, General Harney, commanding the American troops in Oregon and Washington, took possession of San Juan Island on July 27, 1859, by sending Captain Pickett with 461 men to occupy it.

Locally it is called the "Pig War". In 1853, to strengthen the British claim to San Juan Island, which protected the shipping lane to the Fraser River, Governor Douglas had sent John Griffin to establish a Hudson's Bay Company farm on San Juan Island. The American officials, however, considered San Juan Island part of the United States and attempted to collect taxes. In 1858 one of the American settlers, Lyman Cutler, shot a Hudson's Bay Company pig which had been rooting in his potato patch, a trivial incident which brought all the animosity boiling to the surface.

On July 27 the Americans landed troops, on the pretext that American squatters needed protection from the Indians. It was an excuse which touched a sensitive chord, since Governor Douglas was aware of the thousands of American gold seekers who might likewise require protection. The governor responded by sending in ships and men, including Colonel Moody, Lieutenant Lemprière and 14 other Royal Engineers. Rear-Admiral Robert Lambert Baynes restrained Governor Douglas from ordering an attack on the American troops. When General Winfield Scott arrived, it was agreed that British and American troops should both occupy the island until its sovereignty was decided. The joint occupancy lasted for 12 years. The question was finally settled by Kaiser Wilhelm II who on November 25, 1872, handed the disputed islands to the United States.

"The events of that period will still be fresh in the memory of my readers," Lieutenant Mayne wrote in 1862. "It will therefore be remembered how nearly war between the two countries was approached, and by what judicious and timely arrangements it was averted."[22] The incident underlines the importance of the presence of the Royal Engineers in British Columbia, to discourage the idea that the American miners had to be protected from the Indians by American soldiers.

When the arrangements for the joint occupation of San Juan Island were made, the sappers and their officers returned to their peaceable pursuits. In September Charles Wilson recorded that he

Spent a very jolly day at New Westminster. It was something delightful to meet old friends & familiar faces & have a chat over everything, how so & so was getting on & what had become of him; add to which Seddall & Luard are first rate musicians & we had no end of waltzes, galops & songs to enliven us.[23]

At the end of 1859 Mayne was able to report, concerning the Engineers' Camp that "the Engineers, who for some time lived under canvas, are all housed; and commanding a very beautiful view up the river stands a very comfortable house, the residence of their commanding-officer, Colonel Moody." So Mrs. Moody and her growing family were now ensconced in larger quarters and perhaps the colonel could work in peace. "The view of the Fraser from the camp is very pleasing," Mayne continued. "On the left, over Pitt Lake, rise the beautiful peaks known as the Golden Ears; to the right of these, the valley of the Fraser can be traced almost as far as Fort Hope."[24]

By the end of the year the townsites of Yale, Hope and Port Douglas had been surveyed by the Engineers, and streets and building lots laid out. As well, an observatory had been built at the camp and meteorological observations taken, the trail to Burrard Inlet was finished, Lemprière had surveyed the route from Hope to Lytton by way of the Coquihalla, and a road had been built to replace the mule trail between the lakes on the Douglas-Lillooet route.

As Christmas approached and the snow descended from the mountain peaks, the sappers returned from their work to take up winter duties in the camp. The Boundary Commission Engineers stayed on in their forest camps, working to make up for time lost battling the mosquitoes. They had hoped to be in Esquimalt for Christmas, but it was not until December 23 that Wilson wrote "Thaw with a drizzling rain. The work all finished and the first march to winter quarters made, we had a jollification."

December 24th. A beautiful clear day; we were all up at daylight & soon ready for the march. The rain of yesterday had just taken the frost out of the ground & left the prairie in a beautiful state for a gallop & after striking tents and getting the mules started off we went at a racing pace. Lord, whose horse had been lamed, was mounted on a mule & at starting was greatly chaffed, by impertinent

The Boundary Commission working along the 49th parallel.

questions of 'whether he was off for the Darby' or 'going to take a turn in Rotten Row'? but before we had finished the 15 miles he had passed us at a canter with his mule & had all the laugh on his side. We spent a very jolly Xmas even together, the first time we had all dined together for a long time & we drank the health of all at home with loud applause.

December 25th. Alas! Alas! that I should have to say it, but Xmas day is nothing without beef & as we could not get it any other way we killed our cow; our dinner consisted of roast beef, a haunch of venison, ducks, grouse, & a huge plum pudding worthy of old England, which was rather good for a camp dinner.

December 30th. [Esquimalt] Landed at our old barracks &
were very glad to get into comfortable quarters again.[25]

1859 had become history. The Boundary Engineers had
surveyed and cut a satisfactory length of boundary. The
Engineers of the Columbia detachment appeared to be finish-
ing difficult tasks, but Governor Douglas grumbled and the
Colonial Office was not satisfied. In a private letter dated June
21, 1859, Colonel Moody himself suggested that a large portion of the Corps had better be removed.

Chapter Six

1860: "Very Dear Soldiers"

The Royal Engineers of the Columbia detachment were no sooner comfortably housed in their New Westminster camp at the end of 1859 than the Colonial Office considered withdrawing them, concluding that sending them to British Columbia was a "mistake".[1] In the brief time between their departure from England in 1858 and the summer of 1859, the situation in the new colony had changed. The miners were still finding gold, but they had now spread over the province and, since the Ned McGowan "War", did not threaten British sovereignty. The gold rush into the Fraser River included many Americans but there were miners from other countries as well, and as a group they had shown themselves to be law-abiding. Growing numbers of settlers provided a stabilizing influence. The government's gold and land commissioners and magistrates were functioning well and Judge Begbie's justice was viewed with respect. The Royal Navy had sent ships to the west coast and American pressure for expansion northwards had slackened. Only San Juan Island remained a potential trouble spot.

It has been thought that Governor Douglas was somehow responsible for the disbanding of the Royal Engineers in 1863; he was overly critical of them and thought their work could have been performed as well at a lower cost by civil employees, and he considered Colonel Moody extravagant. However, a memorandum from the Colonial Office shows that Governor Douglas was not alone in these views. The memorandum was compiled for the Duke of Newcastle, Secretary of State for the Colonies. The first part of the memorandum, dated April 25, 1860, was written by Henry T. Irving, a secretary. It was sent to his superior, T. Frederick Elliot, Assistant Under-Secretary of State for the Colonies, who added comments before passing it to Chichester Fortescue, Under-Secretary of State for the Colonies, who wrote further comments. Finally it reached the desk of the Duke of Newcastle for a decision. He decided not to take any action until after he had made a visit to Canada, a delay which made possible the further achievements of the Royal Engineers in British Columbia.

Beginning the memorandum, Irving reminded the Colonial Office of the purposes for which the Royal Engineers had been chosen by Lytton. As a military force they were to be used only to repress foreign aggression or in the occasional support of the civil authority, and not as police. They were to act as surveyors, roadmakers and pioneers. The cost of maintaining them was to be borne by the colony from the sale of lands which the Engineers would survey. The pay rates were to be:

Colonel Moody ....£	1,200	per annum
3 Captains, each ....£	350	" "
2 Subalterns, each ....£	250	" "

1 Surgeon....................£   250   "   "

The men: pay varying from 1 to 5 shillings per day per man.

Colonel Moody agreed to remain in the colony one year from the date of his arrival, and then not to quit unless the officer in charge was fully competent. A desire to stay longer was to be communicated to Her Majesty's Government. Irving noted that Colonel Moody had not applied either to stay or to return. The men had been promised grants of land after six years continuous and faithful service.

According to Irving the annual cost of the colonial pay of the party was about £11,000, and the commissariat expenses that much again. The transport, stores and expenses involved in establishing the Royal Engineers in British Columbia amounted to about £40,000.

It was Irving's opinion that the government was not bound to keep the force in British Columbia, and at this point he mentioned that Colonel Moody had already suggested that 50 of the men should be withdrawn. Irving also thought that it was unlikely that the force would be required to repel any foreign aggression, and he suggested that if they were disbanded and located on grants of land, on condition that they perform military service if such was required, they would still provide the moral support of their presence. He pointed out the changed circumstances in the colony: the population of about 6,000 or 7,000 and the considerable naval force at Vancouver Island.

Referring to dispatches from Governor Douglas, Irving noted that many of the men were not available for surveying because of "the necessity of maintaining military discipline, guards, etc." so that the amount of work done was insignificant. "I believe that both the opinions expressed by Governor Douglas and the facts of the case lead to the conclusion that the labor of the Engineers as Surveyors is neither economical nor adapted to a country where rapidity of work is the chief requirement."

The next contributor to the memorandum, Elliot, commented that "They are undoubtedly very dear Soldiers; I cannot help thinking it probable that they are also dear laborers." He referred to a letter from Colonel Moody questioning whether the colony could afford the annual cost of £22,000 for their services. Elliot thought that whatever else should be done, Colonel Moody himself and possibly other officers should be withdrawn, as "there is really no proper work for Colonel Moody at £1200 a year."

Fortescue added his opinion that the Engineers "are an extravagant failure", having spent most of their time laying out townsites and building their own quarters. He considered them "above their work", when "backwoodsmen can do infinitely better."

When the memorandum finally reached the Duke of Newcastle, he wrote:

> I have no doubt that the Engineers in B.Columbia are a "Mistake" and I was meditating their withdrawal when the S.Juan affair broke out. This affair renders a Military force Necessary & I should not feel justified in withdrawing the Engineers without the substitution of another force which I admit might easily be both better and cheaper, but which I see no prospect of obtaining. Upon the whole, though I greatly deprecate this heavy expense for little practical result I fear it must stand over till my return from Canada. I will hope that by that time affairs in S.Juan may have taken a more settled position.

So Lyman Cutler shot the Hudson's Bay Company pig on San Juan Island and the result was a £22,000 annual expense to keep the Royal Engineers in British Columbia for another three years. When the decision to withdraw them was finally made, almost all of the sappers chose to remain in British Columbia. Mrs. Moody wrote in 1859 that she knew of nobody who did not regret coming to the colony, but by 1863 most of the Engineers and their families were content to spend their lives in the new world.

COURTESY OF PROVINCIAL ARCHIVES OF BC

Governor James Douglas.

In the meantime, the cost of the Royal Engineers and Colonel Moody's expenditures worried Governor Douglas. As different as a bull and a racehorse, Douglas and Moody did not work well as a team.

Born in Demerara, British Guiana, of a Creole mother and a Scottish father, James Douglas had spent most of his life in the fur trade. When the North West Company was amalgamated with the Hudson's Bay Company, Douglas transferred his loyalty and obedience to his new masters. He married shy, auburn-haired Amelia Connolly, the half-Indian daughter of Chief Factor William Connolly. It was the custom for the officers to dine together, the junior officers retiring after the toast to the Queen while the senior officers lingered through the evening, smoking their pipes and discussing political, military and scientific matters. Douglas insisted on a certain formality, the table spread with white linen on which stood the crystal decanters. J. S. Helmcken has left a description of Douglas as he appeared from the bottom of the table:

"tall, stout, broad-shouldered, muscular, with a grave bronzed face, but kindly withal."[2] Helmcken admired Douglas and became his son-in-law. A less sympathetic observer saw the governor as slightly ridiculous, with his pompous manner, his uniform, and the orderly who always paced behind him.

In Oregon and Washington, white people were killed by the Indians or Indians slain by American troops or settlers, but in British Columbia the policy of the company and the character of Douglas had inspired the confidence of the Indian people. Lieutenant Mayne wrote, "I for one feel convinced that I should have found it impossible to travel about British Columbia with the ease and freedom from danger which I felt, but for the influence of the Hudson's Bay Company exerted in my favour. The name of Mr. Douglas, as I have more than once said, proved to be a talisman, where it was mentioned, that secured me respect and help."[3]

COURTESY OF PROVINCIAL ARCHIVES OF BC

Judge Matthew Begbie.

In contrast to Douglas, the newly arrived Judge Begbie represented the brilliant, sophisticated world of the Cambridge intellectual. Six foot five inches tall and handsome, he had piercing blue eyes and a pointed waxed moustache, and liked wearing a short dark cloak as he rode a black stallion. On his frequent circuits, he travelled by stage, boat, horse or on foot, sleeping wherever night found him. He would don his wig and robes, open his leather case and hold court in a tent or cabin or even when sitting in the saddle. Graduating from Cambridge at the age of 25, he was almost immediately called to the bar at Lincoln's Inn in London. He had roamed Europe during term holidays, learning languages and sketching. Singer, musician, artist, actor, voracious reader, athlete, Matthew Begbie also loved good conversation. Although he was born into a military family (his father was Colonel T. S. Begbie, a Royal Engineer), his marked aversion to killing prevented a career in the services. Nor could he enter the church, for he had strong doctrinal opinions conflicting with the established church. At the age of 25, when a decision was unavoidable, he became a lawyer. According to his biographer, D. R. Williams, he sought the position of judge in British Columbia "because at the age of 39 he was confident of his ability and still young enough to crave adventure."[4] The correspondence of Solicitor-General Sir Hugh Cairns of August 1858 reveals that "Begbie got the appointment because he was a sound, capable lawyer of integrity."[5]

A fearless judge, he rarely condemned men to hang and had a horror of taking human life; he was never called the "Hanging Judge" in his lifetime. His courage, integrity and energy had a strong influence on the gold rush in British Columbia and the surprising lack of violence is partly the result of his work.

Douglas and Begbie were strong influences on the character of the colony in those crucial first years, but next to them stood Colonel Moody. Douglas's view of Colonel Moody was tersely stated in a letter to the Colonial Office: "The attainments, high moral worth and gentlemanly qualities of Colonel

Moody are familiarly known to his friends. I am in duty bound however to remark that his management as a public administrator in this Colony has not been satisfactory to me."[6] Moody's previous experience in civil administration had been as Governor of the Falkland Islands. Born into a military family, Richard Clement Moody had grown up in various garrison towns. Although he had expensive tastes and tended to ignore details, his love of the new land was genuine and he made grandiose plans for its development. Entering the Fraser River in February 1859, he described the scene to Arthur Blackwood in the Colonial Office;

> The entrance to the Fraser is very striking—Extending miles to the right & left are low marsh lands (apparently of very rich qualities) & yet from the Background of Superb Mountains—Swiss in outline, dark in woods, grandly towering into the Clouds, there is a sublimity that deeply impresses you... I scarcely ever enjoyed a scene so much in my life. My imagination converted the silent marshes into Cuyp-like pictures [a Dutch artist] of horses & cattle lazily fattening in rich meadows in a glowing sunset.[7]

Both his response to the new land and his plans for its future are here revealed. Although he saw himself primarily as a professional soldier, in the letter concerning the Ned McGowan "War" he wrote "I seriously believe I was the most peaceable man on board—Old Soldiers don't play at soldiering."[8] His decision to go on alone to Fort Yale is a demonstration of his courage and when Ned McGowan's men fired over his head, he maintained a mask of calmness. That he fainted when all danger was over is evidence of the hidden strain. Profoundly moved when he conducted the first church service, at Fort Yale, he wrote, "To *me* God in His mercy granted this privilege.... My heart was in the utterance I gave to the beautiful prayers of our Liturgy."[9] Arthur Blackwood of the Colonial Office found Moody to be "always in a hurry & frequently wrong".[10] Enthusiastic to build a beautiful capital city, he ignored Douglas's warnings about the precarious financial situation in the colony.

All three men were religious, their lives set in a Christian context. Although they made mistakes, they possessed an admirable moral rectitude and integrity. British Columbia's history begins with a virgin wilderness, an invasion of gold seekers and three remarkable men. Douglas was the most powerful influence, and Begbie upheld the justice that is a prerequisite for peace, but Lytton's "mistake" of sending Colonel Moody and the Royal Engineers to the colony contributed to the strength of British institutions and character in British Columbia.

Were the Engineers an "extravagant failure"? Possibly the Colonial Office was correct, if the choice of the Engineers for duty in the new colony is judged only in hard economic terms. These men were considered the best soldiers and they were expensive, but their work should not be judged by dollars only. The cool discipline of the small detachment of sappers filing down through the trees to Fort Yale on that frosty January morning in 1859, calmly ignoring the guns being fired by the men at Hill's Bar, reflected the training, pride and discipline they would contribute to the character of the province. There were also many tangible achievements during the three years' grace, 1860 to 1863, earned by the San Juan confrontation.

Chapter Seven

1860: Trails and Roads

Unaware that the Colonial Office was waiting for the right moment to withdraw them, the Royal Engineers carried on their work. In January 1860, Governor Douglas issued a proclamation allowing land to be pre-empted. To register pre-empted land, the Royal Engineers began the work of surveying a road between New Westminster and Vancouver Harbour, and their draughting and record office was enlarged.

Their most urgent task was the construction of trails and roads. Travel patterns had changed since 1858. Before that date, supplies arriving at Fort Langley were taken upriver to Yale and then over the Old Mountain Trail of 1848, crossing the Fraser by raft or boat at Spuzzum. The route then went northwest over the mountains, climbing steeply to avoid the canyon north of Spuzzum, the formidable Nicaragua Bluff (now pierced by Hell's Gate and Ferrabee Tunnels). After 1858 the comparatively limited traffic of the fur traders travelling east of Kamloops was augmented by the thousands of gold seekers, heading north instead of east. The Boston Bar Trail of 1859–60, built by Lemprière and the Royal Engineers, used the Coquihalla and Anderson Rivers to bypass the Fraser Canyon, but this was a longer and higher route, closed for most of the winter. It was obvious that the Fraser River route must be improved.

On January 10, 1860, Governor Douglas asked the Royal Engineers whether they could build a 12-foot-wide, low-level mule trail along the Fraser north of Spuzzum, between Chapman's Bar and Boston Bar. Sapper James Turnbull went upriver to examine the 200-foot sheer Nicaragua Bluff. He considered tunnelling and other options, but chose the cheapest and quickest solution, zigzagging down 500 feet from the elevation of the present highway to the river, then chiselling and blasting a trail around the bluff before zigzagging back up to the original trail. Bids for the work were called in July 1860 and it was completed that same year. This trail had heavy use until it was superseded by the Cariboo Wagon Road of 1863.

Visiting his new diocese, George Hills, the Bishop of British Columbia, recorded his visit to the work at Nicaragua Bluff:

June 12, 1860: I went today to see the works being carried on to form a road through the Canyons, or narrow gorge of the mountains where the Fraser emerges; the object is to get a road for mules round the base of perpendicular rocks. A party of Royal Engineers, assisted by others, are at work blasting the rocks; the work is one of great magnitude, dangerous and arduous of execution. I walked over the narrow ledge round the place at present under the hands of the sappers; along this Indians travel, laden with merchandise, packed with 100 lbs. weight; the footing in some places was certainly not more than half an inch, in one spot a mere in-

dentation for a naked Indian heel, a slip from this would
precipitate down into the abyss of the whirling torrent...
the men were pleased at Mr. Crickmer and myself visiting
these works and treading the critical footholds.[1]

In the early months of 1860, the Boundary Commission
Engineers had to finish their work on the west side of the Cascades before they could move to Fort Colville. Returning to
their earlier camps, they encountered a new danger. Wilson
wrote,

> February 20th. Last night a heavy gale got up & made us all
> feel very uncomfortable. I could not sleep for a long time.
> The night was pitch dark & as I lay on the ground, with my
> buffalo robe round me, I could hear the thundering of the
> trees as they were blown down all round us. In the morning
> we heard the sad news that a tree had fallen on one of the
> tents at a camp about 8 miles off & killed one of the men;
> there were 9 in the tent but by a perfect miracle all escaped
> but one. The gale kept blowing the whole day with great
> violence & we had to go & hold an inquest on the body; so
> mounting our horses, off we went & a rather hazardous
> journey it was, trees falling all round us like nine pins &
> sometimes the tops, broken clean off, would come rattling
> down close beside us, obliging us, as one of our American
> axemen observed, to keep 'our eyes pretty considerably
> skinned' which meaneth to keep our eyes open. . . . This is
> the second man we have lost by falling of trees within 3
> weeks, which has cast a gloom over the whole party.[2]

By March the boundary line was marked from the western
slopes of the Cascades to the sea and they left Fort Langley for
the last time. Back at Esquimalt, Wilson paid a compliment:
"The young ladies here are first rate horse women & sit with
an ease & gracefulness very seldom seen at home even when at
full gallop." On April 28, 1860, the Boundary Engineers de-

parted aboard the *Otter* for Fort Colville which was to serve as the base for the second half of their work.

April 28th. About 6 in the evening we steamed slowly out of Esquimalt Harbour & the three men-of-war there, Ganges, Topaze & Satellite, manned their rigging & gave us three hearty cheers, the bands taking up the air of "Auld lang syne" as we passed each ship; the cheers we returned & were speedily round the corner and out of sight.

May 1st. At 4 in the morning we reached Fort Vancouver, about 90 miles up the [Columbia] river & were received with true English hospitality at the Hudson's Bay Company's fort, one of the gentlemen in charge being a nephew of Mr. Work of Victoria; the fort is now surrounded by the Garrison of American troops under General Harney of San Juan renown. Alas, the poor old fort, once the great depot of all the western fur trade, is now sadly shorn of its glories.

The Engineers went up the Columbia River to The Dalles, portaged, then took another steamer to Walla Walla (Fort Nez Percés). They rode across the treeless desert plain covered with sage bushes. On June 25, Wilson, with old Low, his servant and Sergeant Bigley, the Quartermaster, mounted horses and set off to Fort Colville, "my kit consisting of a buffalo robe & roll of bacon tied up behind the saddle & my gun in front, my dress, moccasins, leather trousers, ditto coat, a flannel shirt & a very old hat." On June 30, they had their first view of the Colville valley, like Shangri-la, where a settlement was comprised of old servants of the Hudson's Bay Company, old trappers, voyageurs, Canadian, French, Iroquois and half-breeds.

June 30th. In the afternoon we found ourselves toiling up a steep hill, on reaching the top of which a view burst on our eyes which I shall never forget. We were on a considerable elevation & far beneath us lay the Colville valley; a small stream winding its way amongst the cornfields of the most luxuriant green & sparkling in the sun like a streak of silver, with the scattered hamlets & dark clumps of trees, formed a scene which of its kind I never saw surpassed.

July 2nd. I rode over 15 miles to the American garrison & back again in the evening. The Americans have got 4 companies of Infantry there, which they sent up last year to protect their Commission from the Indians. The American Commission is now at Pend'Oreille Lake where they have been brought to a stand still by the floods. Our work this year lies east & west from this & by present calculation we expect to finish next year, but I am afraid not in time to get down before the winter which will not bring us home before the spring of '62.

In August Wilson encountered the miners at the Rock Creek gold strike just north of the border. "We were at first taken for custom house officers or gold collectors, who were supposed to be on their way from Fraser river, but after we had explained that we had no connection with the colony, we were most hospitably treated." In fact, Governor Douglas's party did not reach Rock Creek until September 24, journeying over the Dewdney Trail a month after the contract for the building of the trail had been given to Edgar Dewdney, a civil engineer. The trail had been built in order to enable the government to control the new gold mines.

The route which became known as the Dewdney Trail was first examined by Alexander Anderson, then in charge at Fort Alexandria, when the Oregon Treaty closed the old fur brigade road down the Columbia valley. In 1859 Lieutenant Palmer made an official exploration of the route. Early in 1860 Governor Douglas employed Peter O'Reilly, the Gold Commissioner and Magistrate for Fort Hope, to do a further study, and later that year public tenders were called for the construction of "a good mule road from Hope to

The Boundary Commission camp at Haig's pond, between Osoyoos and Rock Creek, on the 49th parallel.

Similkameen".[3] The nine bids received were opened, certified and tabulated by Captain Luard and Captain Parsons on July 4, with young Edgar Dewdney the low bidder at £76 per mile. Walter Moberly was next with a bid of £85 per mile. Dewdney took Moberly as a working partner, and construction of the Dewdney Trail began.

Sergeant William McColl, R.E., was in an advance party, selecting the route for the trail, and Sapper Charles Sinnett kept the field book, from which the plans were drawn. (This is the same man whose print-like penmanship may be admired on the pages of *The Emigrant Soldier's Gazette and Cape Horn Chronicle*). The *Frontier Guide to the Dewdney Trail* details some of the difficulties. Miners and their beasts of burden, or traders taking in supplies, all anxious to get to the new gold-fields of the Similkameen, crowded over the trail, sometimes destroying parts still under construction. Dewdney's decisions about a suitable route occasionally differed from those of the Royal Engineer survey. Dewdney was also upset when Governor Douglas wanted to add 34 miles to the road, at the same price per mile.

During this same busy summer of 1860, Sergeant-Major Cann relocated the trail from Yale to Spuzzum, blasting a pathway suitable for mules. *The New Westminster Times* of October 6, 1860, announced the completion of the task "greatly to the satisfaction of the people of Yale. We believe it is the intention of the merchants and others of that town to give a public dinner, by subscription, to the Royal Engineers employed on the work, to testify to their appreciation of the manner and alacrity with which the work has been carried on."[4] The Yale merchants hoped to recover trade which had been lost when the Boston Bar Trail from Hope (via the Coquihalla and Anderson Rivers) had bypassed them on the east, and the Harrison-Lillooet route had bypassed them on the west.

While Cann's group was working north of Yale, Captain Parsons and a small party of sappers did a reconnaissance survey of the Sumas and Chilliwack country. In the Engineers' camp at New Westminster on September 24, Sapper Henry Smith, who had climbed the hill each morning to make observations in British Columbia's first meteorological station, was married to Miss Sarah Sophia Hill, the school teacher. They were married by the Reverend Mr. Sheepshanks in a tiny church in a field of very large stumps, and when they returned from the church, they were met with music and military honours.

Meanwhile, the Harrison-Lillooet route, which required four separate trips by land interspersed with three voyages by lake steamer, was being improved. The mule trails (two to 3½ metres wide) were being widened into wagon roads (four to five metres in width). Corporal James Duffy was working, during the summer of 1860, in Cayoosh (Lillooet), laying out the townsite so that lots could be sold to settlers. On September 7, Governor Douglas came riding in, inspecting the

Harrison-Lillooet trail. To be sure that the best route for the Second Portage had been chosen, from Lillooet Lake to Cayoosh, Douglas wanted someone to explore an alternative pass, up Cayoosh Creek. When he called for a volunteer, Corporal Duffy, diffident but eager, stepped forward.

On the morning of September 10, he was on his way with a party of Indians, following an Indian trail at a steady eight miles per day, reaching Lillooet Lake on September 16, and returning by a different route. He sent his report to Lieutenant Palmer at Pemberton (at the head of Lillooet Lake); he submitted notes and sketch maps and his opinion that a wagon road was feasible, the greatest obstacle being the rapid drop of 1,000 feet to Lillooet Lake, which could be descended by zigzagging. Having submitted his report, he returned to triangulating with a five-inch theodolite at Cayoosh, and there he found a terse letter awaiting him, from Captain Luard, dated September 26, 1860. "Sapper James Duffy R.E. is desired to explain how it is that he has proceeded upon another service other than the one he was upon without reporting the circumstances to Headquarters. . . . No report has been received as to whether he had completed the duty ordered by Capt. Grant R.E. . . . before volunteering his services to His Excellency the Governor."[5]

His Excellency had in fact written to Colonel Moody on September 8 from Cayoosh, telling him that "I have appointed Corporal Duffy, who very handsomely came forward and volunteered his services, to head the party and report their proceedings. . . . Corporal Duffy, whose conduct on the occasion deserves my thanks, especially looking to the great importance of ascertaining whether this route may not be preferable to the one now in use." Duffy, in his reply to Captain Luard on October 6, explained that "I did not then imagine I was acting wrong in obeying His Excellency."[6] However, the breach of discipline was pursued and Duffy was demoted to Sapper. Perhaps this exchange of letters had less to do with Duffy than with the animosity between Colonel Moody and Governor Douglas.

It would be a consolation to know that Sapper Duffy much enjoyed the exploration for which he eagerly volunteered, for W. T. Balou reported in *The British Colonist* of Friday, January 18, 1861, that "A sapper froze to death on the long portage between Douglas and Cayoosh. His name was James Duffy. Much suffering is experienced in making passage from above to New Westminster. The severest weather I have ever seen on the river I experienced from the sixth to the thirteenth. . . . No express from above, and weather being so bad messengers cannot travel."[7] On a cold January day the entire detachment of Royal Engineers escorted Alice Duffy and the body of Sapper Duffy to the graveyard in New Westminster.

That bitterly cold winter of 1860 found most of the Royal Engineers back in camp at New Westminster. There was a Social Club, and banquets and dances were organized, with

COURTESY OF PUBLIC ARCHIVES OF CANADA

The Boundary Commission at Fort Colville. Mule packed with pork barrels.

Sapper William Haynes conducting the Royal Engineers' band. The Theatre Royale performed comedies and farces. There was skating on the river when it was frozen, and sleighing down Mary Hill after the snow came. It was a healthy life: a medical report for the inhabitants of the Engineers' camp for 1860 stated that "children had been entirely free from the occurrence of measles, scarlatina, whooping cough and other diseases usually befalling their class."[8]

At Fort Colville, across the Cascades, the Boundary Engineers had moved into log huts at the end of November "well mudded on the inside & out & are as warm & comfortable as anyone could wish with a roaring fire inside them",[9] according to Charles Wilson. Unable to work when the snow was deep and the temperature low, they could only await the spring.

December 21st. You can picture the Commission on a winter's evening sitting in a circle round a huge fire of logs, a kettle singing merrily by its side with sundry suspicious looking tumblers standing on a table close by & then the yarns that are told, where everyone has his little troubles & adventures to talk over, of weary nights with mosquitoes, of rattlesnake bed fellows, of onslaughts on grouse, toiling over mountains & fording rapid streams, what one's feelings were when he saw the mule with all his household property go rolling over a precipice, or another's when he broke the stock of his pet double barrel, all is talked & laughed over & often looked back to with a sort of pleasure.

December 25th. We had the Hudson's Bay Company officers to dinner, all Englishmen, & we had a great spread out of beef & plum pudding & broached a small keg of port wine which we had managed to get up for the occasion & with which we drank the health of everybody at home, so that we did not fare badly on the occasion; after dinner we had songs, sentimental & patriotic & innumerable Scotch reels, Highland flings & Mr. Macdonald (in charge of the

H.B.C. fort) gave us a capital sword dance & we then had an amateur Indian war dance and song.[10]

The Christmas before, these Boundary Engineers had had to butcher their own cow for the Christmas feast, and on the Christmas to come they would have no beef at all. However, for most of the Engineers, of both the Columbia detachment and the Boundary Survey, 1860 was a year of hard work and satisfying achievements. The new year would bring the excitement of Lady Franklin's visit.

Chapter Eight

1861: Lady Franklin's Visit

It was Lady Franklin's "ungovernable passion for travel"[1] that brought her to British Columbia in 1861, but it was her niece's letters to her family that made the journey so important. Written by an intelligent observer with a keen sense of humour, Sophia Cracroft's account of their visit to New Westminster describes life in the camp of the Royal Engineers in March 1861.

After Sir John Franklin failed to return from his Arctic explorations, Lady Franklin financed three ventures to supplement those organized by the Royal Navy to search for him. She then sent out the *Fox* in 1859, and this time proof of his death was brought back. At age 68 in 1860, accompanied by her 44-year-old niece, Sophia Cracroft, she set off around the world, first to New York and then, by way of the Panama, to

Victoria, to visit her old friend, Captain George H. Richards, R.N., who had been appointed to the Boundary Commission in 1856.

They arrived in Victoria on February 24, 1861, finding the city's streets a slough of black mud. They wished to visit New Westminster and the Fraser; as Captain Richards could not accompany them because of "some unexpected Boundary Commission work", and Lieutenant Mayne could not be spared from his duties, Second Lieutenant Hankin, R.N., became their escort. Aboard the *Otter*, they travelled through the Gulf Islands.

> We emerged into the open Strait (called the *Gulf* of Georgia) through a very narrow channel (nearly opposite to the mouth of the Fraser) which ought to bear no other name than "Plumper Pass" given by Captn Richards who surveyed it, but (Yankeelike) the American Boundary Commissioner, wrote to him, claiming that it shd receive the name of the "Active" an American vessel which (he said) had been the first to go through it.... [Captain Richards] ascertained that the "Active" had not been in that channel at all, but in a neighbouring one!

At the dock at New Westminster, Captain Parsons and Captain Gosset awaited them, quickly transferring the two ladies to the Engineers' boat to transport them to the camp near Sapperton. Sophia Cracroft described the camp:

> We were struck with the appearance of order in the arrangement of the buildings in the "Camp." Every house was of course of wood, but the designs shewed all the taste & skill which might be looked for from a party of Engineers.... Col. Moody has with great wisdom built a thoroughly good house, as substantially as a wooden one can be, and with large well-proportioned rooms, quite in contrast with every house we have yet seen except the Governor's in Victoria. It was cheaply done, if the difficulties

and high rate of labour be taken into consideration, for it only cost £1000. There are three large sitting rooms on the ground floor with a good passage, kitchen &c and 4 very good bedrooms over—with offices all well enclosed and thoroughly finished—everything of wood, except of course the chimneys. It was several months building for a reason characteristic of the country. It was unfortunately begun in the spring—the usual period arrived for the reign of mosquitoes, and it was impossible to go on with the work until they had taken their departure after the heat of the summer had passed away . . . they absolutely blacken the walls of the room. . . . People who *can* leave New Westminster in the summer, always do so, to escape this terrible scourge: but happily it is curing itself by degrees, as the forest is being cut down.

It had been arranged that Lady Franklin and Sophia Cracroft would go upriver to Fort Yale in the *Maria*, with Captain Irving in charge. They arrived in New Westminster on March 5, and returned to the capital the next day, to board the steamer.

The Engineers' Camp, New Westminster. The Moodys' house is on the left.

Before starting in the boat for N.Westminster we walked about the Camp, admiring the taste & order which reigns throughout it. All the buildings are different & in thoroughly good taste. The paths are neat & straight & of course the people (being soldiers) look less rough than the usual population. The Engineers are 120 in number, all volunteers, come out for 6 years. [At New Westminster] the forest was formerly so dense that only 18 months back one of the Engineer officers lost his way in trying to get from N.Westminster to the Camp—had to climb down the bank & get into a canoe & so make his way home.

Miss Cracroft was also told about the church in New Westminster:

The service receives an very important addition from the Engineers. The Harmonium is played by Dr. Seddall, who also leads the choir consisting in great measure of other members of the Corps. The music is said to be exceedingly good.

Arriving at Yale, which "looked rather dreary, and was in a perfect sop of mud", they visited ashore but decided to keep their staterooms on the *Maria*. On Saturday, March 9, 1861:

It had been arranged the evening before, that we were to be taken up the river in a canoe through a fine pass known only by the Spanish term of Canon (pronounced Canyon) up to some Falls. Mr. Dallas had sent up an order for this, to the H.B.Co's agent here; and at 10 o'clock, one of the largest canoes was waiting for us, which on entering, we found to be manned by 12 Indians, all dressed in red woollen shirts, with gay ribbons in honor of my Aunt. They rowed of course in the Indian fashion, with short paddles, 5 at one end, 5 at the other, with one man standing in the bow, the other at the stern—we seated in the middle. . . . On our left (right bank of the river) a road is being made along the face of the hill by the Engineers of N. Westminster, involving blasting, bridging ravines, & scientific levelling. It was a portion of it that Capt. Parsons was come to inspect and he was now at his work.

Lady Franklin did not have the opportunity to actually see the road under construction, but Bishop Hills, also travelling along the Fraser River that summer, recorded some of the dangers of the work:

We came to the Thompson. A crowd of packed animals were waiting on the other side to cross the ferry . . . the road is bad and frequently dangerous. We ascended sometimes to a great height on the almost perpendicular side of the mountain, on which a false step would precipitate anyone to destruction. To-day we met a man with a pack team in a gloomy mood; he has just been afflicted with the sight of one of his animals rolling over and down the side, dashing from crag to boulder, until the mighty torrent below received it on its heaving bosom and hurried it away. To us, about to pass the same road, this information, though useful as a warning, was not very consolatory.

Captain Grant and Lieutenant Palmer received us with their usual courteous hospitality. They dine at the same time with the men; so we sat down at their midday meal, and enjoyed a hearty repast. It is interesting to see the wonderful change produced in a country by roads.[2]

While Lady Franklin and Miss Cracroft were upriver, a surprise had been prepared for them:

[Returning], we pulled back easily, the current carrying us down with great rapidity, and our boatmen began again to sing in chorus, or rather one gave a sort of recitative (which we were told set forth the charms of their vocation) echoed in chorus by the rest, whose lungs seem to be in excellent order. On reaching the narrowest part of the Canon, we beheld (suspended from the rafters of a salmon drying shed) a long pole stretching over the stream, on which was hung a white banner with the words "Lady Franklin Pass" printed in large letters. The Indians stopped their paddling and we were told that this name was bestowed by the inhabitants of Yale in honor of my Aunt's visit, the said inscription being saluted from the opposite bank, by dipping a flag (the Union Jack) 3 times.

Safely back at Yale, they entered a shop so that Lady Franklin could buy each of the Indian paddlers a gay cotton handkerchief "& they were also to have a good feast of bread, well smeared with treacle." On Monday, March 11, back at the Royal Engineers' Camp at New Westminster, they dined alone with the Moodys. They had met Governor Douglas: "All people speak with great admiration of the Governor's intellect—and a remarkable man he must be to be thus fit to govern a colony.... His manner is singular... there is a gravity, & a something besides which some might & do mistake for pomposity, but which is the result of long service in the H.B.Co's service." During the next four days, Lady Franklin and Miss Cracroft participated in the life of the camp:

There is a smooth & well raised path upon the river in front of the Camp from Col. Moody's house (wh stands at the end of the buildings), passing the offices, storehouses, theatre, barracks &c &c and running off (past the pretty little house of Captn. & Mrs. Grant) into a trail, or road, which the Engineers have made to the Burrards Inlet about 5 miles off. Upon the pathway, Mrs. Moody takes her 5 children day by day, & Mrs. Grant her 2 little ones. Each lady has to be her own head nurse, if not sole nurse.... Mrs. Moody & Mrs. Grant each has her baby to carry but are often relieved by a stray gentleman; & the babies are quite used to this. It is quite common to see gentlemen carrying the children, out of natural pity for the mothers.

Captain John Grant, RE.

On Wednesday, March 13, having declined to accompany the officers on what must have been a cold and damp picnic, Lady Franklin and Sophia Cracroft "tramped on in the rain" touring the "multifarious divisions" of the Camp.

Col. Moody took us to the printing press, where the work is done to perfection, the Printer [Richard Wolfenden] being a very able man and keeper also of all the Camp accounts. Then we went into the offices where all the map making goes on. The Engineers survey the country & make the maps from their observations—plotting, it is called, and most beautiful is their work, entirely done by hand, with the finest pen. They also make plans, and architectural drawings. One man has charge of certain instruments with which he takes stated observations & works out the results. The corps is one of picked men, who are continually adding

to their acquirements, by the work they are employed in, &
by the use of their opportunities. They have an excellent
Library of their own, stocked with first rate books in
science, History (military & civil) & general literature.
They have their own club & reading room (in the theatre)
for which they take in some newspapers from Engd and
Scotland. So it is not very wonderful that they should be
the very superior men we perceived them to be. The
theatre (built entirely by themselves) is a very nice little
place, with a well raised stage and a regular orchestra. At
the upper end (over the entrance) is a gallery where the officers & ladies sit, leaving the whole of the floor to the men
and their friends. Our fine weather was gone, & we
tramped on in the rain to the multifarious divisions into
workshops, stores, mess rooms, barracks &c which make a
Camp a community complete in itself—and we ended by
the officers quarters & mess room (they were away on a picnic to which they had invited us) & especially the rooms of
Dr. Seddall who has a quantity of Indian curiosities which
he invited us to see. A large painted mask was exceedingly
good, & also some of the carvings, but they were not new to
us.

Friday, March 15. The soldiers are going to get up a play
tomorrow evening for my Aunt. It cannot take place earlier
on account of the absence of many of the men from the
Camp until Saturday afternoon. Some of the best actors are
working on the road to Burrard's Inlet, which is to be finished today.

Saturday, March 16. We dined early so as to give the
soldier servants time to be present in the theatre at 7—and
we found the room quite full, most of the women having
their babies & children with them—& very well the little
creatures behaved. One thing in their favor was that there
were few strange faces, the Camp being like one great family.

The Royal Engineers presented two plays, "Ben Bolt" and "Sent to the Tower".

The most amusing thing was the women, men in disguise of course, with, as it happened, the gruffest voices you can imagine! Ben Bolt's Ladye love covered up his whiskers with long black curls, but notwithstanding was certainly no type of feminine grace. The other woman was a wife & mother and wore a cap—moreover she was not apostrophised by a love, as in the other case. I fancy these two men do all the female parts, having shaved their moustaches for the purpose! The scenes are all painted by one of the soldiers & very well they are done, especially the drop scene, an Italian view. The orchestra numbered seven instruments & very well they played. At the end of the first piece some of them slipped out, as they were the singers. They first gave us "Here in Cokol Grot" which they sung beautifully, without accompaniment. The curtain fell & a hornpipe began & on the curtain rising agin, Mr. Hankin bounded on the stage in full sailer's costume (all white and blue), flung down his hat, folded his arms, & danced his hornpipe BEAUTIFULLY. You can image the reception he got from the astonished audience. He was encored & very good naturedly came on again. He had slipped out of his place in the gallery with us, & Mrs. Moody had noticed to me that she supposed R. Seddall wanted to have him near himself to pay him off, for what do you think? The last of his pranks had been to take the Doctor's red beard in one hand & the scissors in the other, from which he proceeded to cut it off, & lay it on the table before the poor Doctor's eyes!

This was the second time Dr. Seddall suffered the loss of his much prized, silky red beard. Philip Hankin, the culprit, was a young man of 25, a sub-lieutenant in the *Plumper* who later left the Royal Navy for colonial service on Vancouver Island.

The activities in the Engineers' Camp, observed by Sophia Cracroft, have been summarized by Major Veitch, a Royal Canadian Engineer:

All the maps of that time they drew, lithographed and printed in Sapperton. They formed the Lands and Works Department; they established the Government Printing Office and printed the first British Columbia Gazette. They inaugurated the first building society on the mainland, the first social club on the mainland, the first theatre and theatrical society on the mainland. They designed the first schoolhouse. They designed and built the first Protestant church on the mainland—the church of St. John the Divine—originally at Langley and now at Maple Ridge and they designed other churches—the original Holy Trinity, New Westminster, St. Mary's, Sapperton and probably those at Yale, Hope and Douglas. They designed the first coat of arms of the Colony. They designed the first postage stamp. [The Royal Engineers were disbanded before the first postage stamp was designed, but it may have been the work of J. B. Launders, R.E.] They established the first observatory where they kept continuous scientific meteorological observations.... They had the first private hospital and the first private library, both of which were later to benefit the citizens of New Westminster. And indirectly they built the first Parliament buildings, for on 21st January, 1864, the first session of the first Legislative Council of the Colony of British Columbia opened in the then vacant barracks of the Royal Engineers at Sapperton, New Westminster.[3]

What is surprising is not that the Engineers are responsible for all these "firsts" but that their achievements are largely forgotten. More than 50 drawings, preserved in the Provincial Archives, demonstrate their design and drafting skills, in plans for the gold assay office, jail, barracks and officers' quarters, customs house, hospital, pier, bridges, mint, treasury building, school, churches, and Colonel Moody's house, all of which were built in New Westminster. Most of their designs have a spartan simplicity, suited to the limited means of the young colony, but the church and Colonel Moody's house expressed the Victorian Gothic mode. Unfortunately, neither of these buildings has survived. Drawings of the house show the steep Gothic roof, bay windows and the attached veranda characteristic of this style. In three existing churches, designed and built by the Royal Engineers, at Hope, Yale and Sapperton, one can experience an English parish church transferred to the new world, using local materials and craftsmanship.

The town plans (New Westminster, Hope, Yale, etc.) were drawn and lithographed at the Camp printing office, supervised by Captain Parsons. The chief draftsman was Sapper James Launders. The 17-year-old bugler, Robert Butler, who had pursued the murderer on the Harrison trail, worked in the printing office in the winter. Lady Franklin and Sophia Cracroft were shown the small Columbian Press, used to print the first newspaper in British Columbia, the *British Columbia Gazette*.

The first New Westminster newspaper, *The British Columbian*, has left another glimpse of the Engineers in 1861. In February, just before the arrival of Lady Franklin and Sophia Cracroft, the Engineers helped to clear a cricket ground. The reporter wrote that about a hundred Royal Engineers "accompanied by their band, marched to the field of battle" and attacked the trees. There were almost as many New Westminster citizens there to share the work, and two colossal fires raged, towers of flame and smoke. "Shortly after two o'clock, His Excellency accompanied by Colonel Moody came upon the ground." At five o'clock the Engineers retired to the Camp. "In the evening, Capt. Bullen of the steamer *Hope* kindly made it known that he would carry down from the camp all those who wished to go to the city to finish the day by a dance. Accordingly that steamer brought down a perfect crowd of men, women and children who adjourned to

Mr. Hick's new Hall and enjoyed themselves till ten o'clock,
when Capt. Bullen again placed his steamer at their service
and took them to the camp."[4]

Sophia Cracroft's journal only briefly mentions the primary
task of the Engineers: road building. In 1861 the Engineers
transformed the 1859 trail, running from their camp to Port
Moody, into a wider wagon road. Gibraltar Hill, on the
Harrison-Lillooet route, was improved by Sergeant
Bridgeman, but at the same time, the high cost of freighting
on this road, with its three lake sections, made it essential to
improve the route along the Fraser. In this same year,
Sergeant McColl and a party of sappers, dispatched to find
the best site for a bridge to replace the ferry crossing, chose a
spot just north of Spuzzum. With miners still moving into the
Similkameen and Rock Creek area, Governor Douglas ordered that Dewdney's mule trail be widened to a wagon road;
83 sappers with 50 civilians began the task, working east from
Hope, under Captain Grant, who has been called "the
greatest roadbuilder of them all."[5] Colonel Moody spoke of
"Captain Grant's known energy."[6] Captain Grant and his
men completed 25 miles of road before winter, but they never
returned to the project. When the Rock Creek gold quickly
played out, the miners departed for more lucrative fields. In
the following year, all money and men were required for the
building of the Cariboo Road.

Although the work of the detachment appeared to be going
well, the displeasure of the Colonial Office hung over Colonel
Moody. Relations with Governor Douglas deteriorated. Not
only worried about the expenses of the Royal Engineers, the
governor was exasperated by the difficulties of not knowing
what monies were being spent or committed by the colonial
treasurer and postmaster, Captain William Driscoll Gosset,
R.E. In a confidential report, after Gosset's departure on sick
leave in 1862, Governor Douglas gave the Colonial Office his
opinion of the man:

As a financial officer he was valueless. I have invariably

found him defective in judgement. His temper is capricious, and I cannot recall a single instance of any useful suggestion emanating from him. I could never rely on his cordial co-operation, where combined action was necessary, and I am persuaded that he encouraged disaffection and wilfully misrepresented my government through the Public Press, both in this country and in Europe. In short I believe him to be politically faithless and unprincipled.[7]

Gosset, a close personal friend of Colonel Moody, had been seconded from the Royal Engineers to serve as colonial treasurer and postmaster. Given the responsibility for the Assay Office and Colonial Mint, built by the Royal Engineers, Gosset in 1862 struck off a number of $10 and $20 gold coins, against the orders of Governor Douglas. However, when Gosset returned to England at the end of 1862 he was promoted to the rank of major, and thereafter rose through the ranks to become a major-general in 1873.

Criticized by both the Colonial Office and the governor, Colonel Moody took his family to Victoria in June 1861, for a month's holiday from the mosquitoes and other problems. Mrs. Moody wrote to her mother that "Richard is not at all brisk just now I am sorry to say he has such constant headaches."[8]

In 1861 the Engineers of the Boundary Survey completed their work, but too late to get out of Fort Colville before the winter imprisoned them. There were some diversions. Charles Wilson wrote to his sister about,

A grand ball up at the Hudson's Bay fort given by Mr. Macdonald, at which all the beauty and fashion of the place was present, all the old trappers & voyageurs of the Company drove over in their sleighs . . . some of the Canadian boat songs sung by a lot of voyageurs were capital. . . . At 4 o'clock in the morning I found myself dancing a 'reel de deux' with an Indian squaw, in a state of uncertainty as to whether I had any legs on at all, having danced them clear away & nearly dislocated them into the bargain by trying to pick up the proper step, a kind of spasmodic kick in which the legs are doubled up & thrown out again in the most extraordinary manner.... We all enjoyed ourselves excessively.[9]

The Engineers finally reached the watershed, the continental divide in the Rockies where their work would be finished. In midsummer, Wilson got his first view of the central plains of the continent:

July 31st. Three of us started off to pay our devoirs to the final monument on the boundary. After a short scramble we got on the summit or divide, some distance north of the line, the divide being at that point comparatively low and

COURTESY OF PROVINCIAL ARCHIVES OF BC

The boundary line between the United States and British Columbia.

covered with grass. . . . Leaving the grassy ridge, we commenced a fresh ascent and after a good climb over bare rock
where hands and feet were well employed, a steady eye
needed and an occasional halt to watch the course of a stone
sent rolling by the foot into a little lake some 1500 feet below us, we stood on the narrow shoulder beside the Cairn
of stones which marked the end of our labours and here we
found tokens of previous visitors in the shape of sundry
Anglo Saxon names engraved on the stones, to which truly
English record we refrained from adding ours. The view
from this point was very fine, precipices and peaks, glaciers
and rocks all massed together in such a glorious way, that I
cannot attempt to describe it.

As the year 1861 approached its close, and the pressure to
complete the boundary work on schedule increased, some of
the men fell ill. On November 18, Dr. Lyall was unable to
continue his work and returned to Victoria, and Bauerman
left with ten men for England. "The constant exposure and
wear and tear has told pretty heavily on some of our party and
they have been sent away to escape our rough winter." Their
work was completed but being unable to depart until spring,
they appear to have spent a rather dreary Christmas in camp.

Our cook having cleverly contrived to boil up his pipe and
tobacco with the soup, we spent a rather cheerless Xmas
eve and everyone went to bed at an early hour, with vastly
unpleasant sensation.

1862 would see many of them back at home in England (although some of them chose to transfer to the Columbia
detachment in order to remain in British Columbia). 1862 was
also to be the year of the Cariboo gold rush and the year when
the Engineers undertook their most memorable task, the construction of the Cariboo Road.

Chapter Nine

1862: The Cariboo Road

Although the "rush" to the Cariboo occurred in 1862, the gold had been discovered there much earlier. When "Doc" Keithley and George Weaver made the first important strike at Keithley Creek in 1860, traders, packers, tavern-keepers, and miners flocked in. Other rich strikes followed. Escaping the intense cold of winter in the interior in 1861, 2,000 miners brought out their gold and came to Victoria, again a tent city. However, in the Cariboo most of the gold was found deep underground, requiring 40- or 50-foot shafts, water-wheels, pumps, and hoisting-gear. This meant that mining became capitalized and poor miners were forced to build roads, become traders or farmers, or depart for home. The strikes in the Cariboo had been well publicized in *The Times* of London, and the discovery of the gold of Williams Creek, which exceeded all other sites for quantity and value, attracted men from Europe, the British Isles and eastern Canada. When the value of the gold topped the $4,500,000 mark and there were revenues to the colony from customs duties, tolls, miners' licences and the sale of lands, Governor Douglas decided that the colony could well afford to borrow £50,000 pounds to build a road to the goldfields through the Fraser Canyon.

In a speech given in 1908, the road builder Walter Moberly said that he and Colonel Moody had several interviews with Governor Douglas early in 1862 and "we managed to convince him that the Yale-Cariboo route was the best to adopt for the general development of the country and that it was imperative that its construction should be undertaken at once."[1] A wealthy merchant, Charles Oppenheimer, and a friend of his, T. B. Lewis, joined Moberly to apply for a charter to build this road, provided that they got the right to collect tolls and that there was a financial subsidy from the government for the cost of construction. Having already applied for a loan from the British government, and feeling certain that the money would be available, Governor Douglas granted the charter. Later in the year, when the money was not forthcoming and the workmen were clamouring for their pay, the charter was withdrawn. Moberly suffered severe financial losses and Oppenheimer fled to the United States to escape arrest. Moberly did not blame the governor, "as I had been the principal cause of leading Governor Douglas to undertake this great work which had placed him in a very serious dilemma."[2]

The road was to be built in sections: Captain Grant and the Royal Engineers, with some civilian labour, were to build from Yale to Chapman's Bar; Joseph Trutch would build, by contract, from Chapman's Bar to Boston Bar; Thomas Spence was to construct the section from Boston Bar to Lytton; and Oppenheimer, Moberly and Lewis would construct the section north from Lytton to connect with the wagon road to be built by G. B. Wright south from Fort Alexandria.

A quantity of supplies and tools was easily shipped to Yale, but there were neither enough boats nor pack animals to get the freight to Lytton; large numbers of Indians were engaged to pack the supplies on their backs. At Yale Moberly found men looking for road work, but as they were without money, food, clothing or boots, he had to advance them part of their wages before they could start for Lytton on foot. When news of the rich strikes in the Cariboo came down the road, some of those men, indebted to Moberly, deserted the project, and were replaced by Chinese labourers who worked industriously and faithfully. As no saddle horses were available at Yale, Moberly arrived at Lytton with sore and blistered feet. Work camps were established and soon the picks and shovels were biting into the rough terrain.

In May 1862, Captain Grant was ordered to begin work, with 53 sappers, on the first, worst section, the six miles from Yale north. A trail already existed there, which Miss Cracroft had noted in her journal of March 1861, but now solid rock walls would have to be blasted and cribbing constructed. The Royal Engineers were also to build another difficult piece, the nine miles from Cook's Ferry (Spence's Bridge) along the Thompson River. The remainder of the road would be let out on contract to civilians who were paid with cash or the right to collect tolls.

A month before the order came to begin the Cariboo Road, the Engineers of the Boundary Commission were at last able to depart from Fort Colville. In the words of Charles Wilson:

April 2nd. We left our barracks at Colville, four years to the very day from the date of our leaving England and travelled about 10 miles. There was an immense assemblage of Indians to see us out, and a great deal of shaking hands gone through.[3]

On May 13 they were back in Esquimalt where they quickly cleared their camp and boarded ship for home. As he sailed southwards, Wilson wrote that "We left Victoria with regret. My sojourn there will always be amongst my pleas-antest reminiscences. I have a great wish to return."⁴ But Charles Wilson did not come back.

From Point Roberts to the continental divide of the Rocky Mountains, approximately 400 miles, the surveyors had cleared about 190 miles of corridor along the parallel, leaving the rest untouched because it was inaccessible. The cutting was done at intervals, in strips of about half a mile, 20 feet wide on each side of the boundary. The line was marked at intervals of about a mile and a half between Semiahmoo and the Whatcom trail with iron markers four feet high and six inches square, marked on one side "Treaty of Washington" and on the other "June 15, 1846", each weighing about a hundred pounds. Other points were marked by pyramids of stones six or eight feet high. It was decided that the spot where the 49th parallel met the sea, at Point Roberts, should be marked by a stone cairn, and the contract was given to E. Brown of New Westminster. The cost of the survey to the British government is unknown; the United States spent $595,233.03. After investing much money in the project, both the British and the American governments lost the reports of their separate Boundary Commissioners. New settlers discovered that in places three lines had been cut through the woods, and sometimes there were two sets of stone cairns, but the survey reports which explained these anomalies were nowhere to be found, in London or Washington.

Would the work have to be completely redone? This question was being asked when, in 1898, Otto Klotz, astronomer for the Canadian government, while visiting the Greenwich Observatory Library near London, happened to notice two green boxes on a high shelf. The letters B.N.A. caught his eye, which he interpreted as "British North America". As no one knew what the boxes contained, a ladder was produced and the boxes brought down and dusted. When a lid was removed "there lay before my bulging eyes the records of the 49° parallel west of the Rocky Mountains—the records that had been looked for the past thirty years! A happy man was

I.''⁵ The presence of extra lines and stone cairns was a result of the difficulties of ascertaining latitude in mountainous regions, where deflection of the plumb line is due to the anomalous distribution of matter. Where the American and British line differed, the officers of the two commissions agreed that a mean parallel should be adopted and a new line was run and marked.

As the Boundary Commission detachment sailed home to England, unaware that their work was about to be lost for almost 40 years, the Columbia Engineers continued their work. In the summer of 1862, the Fraser Canyon reverberated with dynamite explosions. On Friday, June 27, 1862, Bishop George Hills found himself in the middle of road construction:

> We left our camp at nine o'clock, and reached the formidable mountain called the Jackass, from the propensity of mules to fall over and be lost upon its dangerous and steep pathways. The especial difficulty now was the blasting operations of the roadmakers, high up on the mountain side, from which came down, with tremendous force and fury, whole avalanches of rocks and smaller debris, shooting over and past the trail, and utterly blotting it out. We were told we could pass when the workmen ceased their labours for the day; so we waited patiently, and about seven o'clock started to cross this dangerous point. On coming up to where the road was, I saw at once there was great risk for our animals, which would, having to cross the mass of loose stones, be sure to lose their footing and probably be rolled over with their packs; so I determined to take the lower trail, which, though very bad, avoided that particular difficulty. It had, however, its own difficulties, which I had investigated earlier in the day, under the guidance of an Indian who declared it safe even while the blasting was going on. A huge rock, however, precipitated from above, some twenty yards ahead only of the spot where I stood, made me conclude it would not be safe until the blasting was

over. That being now the case, we proceeded. . . . The train passed on, missed a turning upon which they should have gone, and went forward to a most dangerous and impassable trail—a mere Indian footway, now disused. As soon as I found out the mistake, I stopped them; and there we were in most imminent danger. The narrow pathway, on which ten horses (seven of them bearing packs) and six men were now standing, had not in some portions of it ten inches of footing. Above was the perpendicular mountain and below was a chasm down to the torrent, some 800 feet. What was to be done? . . . By God's great mercy, we succeeded in turning each horse, and after considerable anxiety and exertion regained the right path and continued our journey till dark, when we camped at a sweet spot.[6]

The Cariboo Road, between Yale and Spuzzum.

The construction of a wagon road from Lillooet to Fort Alexandria on the Fraser south of Quesnel was the task of Sergeant-Major John McMurphy, one of the heroes of Sebastopol, during the Crimean War. Almost 50 years old and one of the oldest men in the detachment, he had five medals to speak for his courage and initiative. Ordered to Lillooet to take charge of the construction of the Lillooet-Fort Alexandria road, McMurphy kept a journal of his work. This small notebook, now one of the treasures of the Royal Engineers' Museum at Vedder Crossing, is written in a neat, precise, readable hand. *En route* to Lillooet on the Harrison-Lillooet road, McMurphy began:

May 26th, 1862: Embarked on Steamer Moody at New Westminster for service on the road from Lillooet to Mud Lake.

May 28th: Started on the stage at 7 a.m. for Tennasse Lake. Arrived 8 p.m.

May 29th: Took the steamer for Pemberton at 11 a.m. and arrived about 7 p.m. the same day.[7]

After waiting for repairs to the Anderson Lake steamer, McMurphy and his men crossed the lake by steamer in four hours, then made their way to Seton Lake, and another four-hour voyage. From the north end of Seton Lake they walked, arriving in Lillooet the next day. Lillooet was Mile 0 on the wagon road they were to build, an extension of the Harrison-Lillooet route. Pack trains frequently filed past the men as they worked:

June 7th: A large train with provisions and iron work for the steamer that is being built near Alexander. A great many miners passed this way today also. There has been a good many miners returned today also who say the snow is too deep, and flour selling for 5s a pound.

June 10th. Train of ten beasts passed today from Salmon River. Drivers state the Californians are leaving it for Cariboo, a great many miners have gone up today, principally Canadians. A case of Brandy and a box of preserves for our gruel arrived as we complained having nothing to eat but beans and bacon three times a day which is a very good thing now and then, but 21 times a week is too often.

June 22nd. Rode across the mountain [Pavilion] and had a look at every corner of it where it was possible to bring the road and decided that a good grade of 1 in 10 can be gotten with little trouble, at the same time condemned a bridge of 90 ft. that was nigh finished, as it had neither strength nor anything else about it that could recommend it.

Most of the actual construction of the road was done by contractors. The width of the road was about 5½ metres; if the work was satisfactory, McMurphy gave them a certificate which they then presented to the government for payment. The most difficult part of the road was the descent down the north side of Pavilion Mountain where the road required considerable cribbing.

July 17th: It is a first rate road both in grades and finish. Everyone says the mountain is the best part of the road. There was 211 beasts passed this way today. There was 2 wagons arrived at our camp today one with 5 pair of oxen, drawing 2 tons. The other with 3 pair drawing 50-hundred weight and came out there they say quite easy.

July 19th: The road going well, a large train of 106 mules passed up this morning from Lytton, having come through Fountain Gap. Muleteers say packers from the other side [the Thompson River] will all come this way when they hear of such a good road and such good feed for their cattle.

Sergeant-Major John McMurphy, RE.

August 9th: Started at 5 AM from the Hay Ranch and met Capt. Parsons about 9 AM. Returned in Capt. Parson's company to camp in the evening, and I was well pleased to hear Capt. Parsons express himself so well pleased at the Road as we rode along, but when I was told that he was Inspecting Officer, the handsome manner he spoke of my trouble in bringing the road thro such a difficult part, and the marked improvement seen on the Road since I joined, made me think that my care and trouble was all as nothing since I had got my Officer's Approval.

Bishop Hills returned over Jackass Mountain in September 1862 and reported that the new road was completed except for a couple of bridges. Near Chapman's Bar he had a narrow escape:

To travel this road while blasting is going on is not free from danger. Sunday, near Chapman's Bar, I was riding along the trail, elevated perhaps 100 feet from the river, and as I arrived on a small bridge over a chasm, an explosion took place immediately beneath my feet. I was enveloped in smoke, and debris were scattered around and over me. My horse happily was quiet, otherwise the least start would have cast me headlong over the edge, which is unprotected, and I should have been dashed upon the rocks below. I of course expected masses of the rock to come upon my head. I escaped; and, on passing round about thirty yards, found the blasters in a place of safety, they having fled, after firing the fuse, from the very spot which I occupied when the explosion took place. They were not a little surprised to see me.[8]

On the Lillooet road, when the gold of late autumn brightened the canyon and the nights were freezing cold, McMurphy was beginning to think about closing down the work:

October 8th: Snow fell last night. Threatening for more. 2 miners passed this AM with 12,000 dollars each from Williams Creek.[9]

This journal records a small part of the gold rush traffic moving into the interior of the colony and explains the urgency and importance of the Engineers' road work. At this time Lillooet's population approached 15,000, making it the second-largest town north of San Francisco. Some settlers had already established farms along the route, growing vegetables to sell to the miners. McMurphy's October 8 reference to the gold coming down the road explains why the contractors had trouble keeping men at road building for a wage of only $54 per month. Leaving the road unfinished, McMurphy closed the last camp on November 29 and returned to New Westminster.

No doubt through the winter the Engineers discussed Moberly's problems with the Cariboo Road. When the Colonial Office failed to lend money for the work, Governor Douglas arranged a loan of $50,000 from the Bank of British Columbia, which had just opened for business in the colony. With $6,000 in cash and the promise of more, Moberly returned to Lytton. No sooner had he arrived there than he received a letter from a friend, by special messenger, informing him that the government would not send him the remaining $44,000, that he was to be arrested for the non-payment of an account due in Victoria, and that a writ had been obtained to cancel the charter which

> had been forfeited as the work was not going on properly.... This unscrupulous act on the part of the Government I afterwards found out was owing to the refusal of the Imperial Government to grant a large loan to the colony upon which Governor Douglas relied for building the Yale-Cariboo road and the extension of the Harrison-Lillooet road northerly from Lillooet, and as I was the one to whom the largest amount would have to be paid it was decided to sacrifice me and carry the other contractors through, especially as the Government would gain a large and very expensive portion of the constructed road I had built without paying anything for it, which was a very convenient and profitable thing for them, but it was a disgraceful and dishonest transaction on their part.[10]

Captain Grant was sent to deal with Moberly. Before his arrival, Moberly borrowed a few hundred dollars to pay the amount for which he had been arrested. Moberly relinquished to Captain Grant his charter rights, the supplies (tents, tools, etc.) and Captain Grant agreed to pay the wages of the men and the sub-contracts Moberly had let.

Captain Grant and myself now proceeded to my different road camps of which I put him in full possession, and when everything was out of my hands Captain Grant proposed that he should appoint me to carry on the works for the Government for the rest of the season. This proposition I was glad to accept for I had not a dollar left, and then Captain Grant told the men that from that time they would be paid their wages by the Government and that I was in full charge of the works, and furthermore that he would do his utmost to get their back wages paid, but he could not absolutely promise more as that matter rested with Governor Douglas. Those wages were ultimately paid in full; they amounted to about $19,000. When this business was closed up at the end of the year, the country had gained a large and most expensive portion of the Cariboo wagon road built, which cost them nothing, but it left me a ruined man with heavy personal liabilities, which took all the money I could make during eight subsequent years to finally pay off.[11]

In the Engineers' Camp that autumn, they talked also about Lieutenant Palmer's summer reconnaissance to determine if there was a shorter route to the Cariboo by sea to Bentinck Arm, up the Bella Coola valley and across the interior plateau to Williams Lake. An account of his explorations survives in an interview with his widow, Mrs. Mary Spencer Palmer, which appeared in *The Daily Colonist* in 1930. She spoke of the "adventures of my gallant husband ... when we and the country were young", and continued,

It was in 1862, before our marriage. He bade me goodbye, telling me he had been detailed to continue his work of finding a new route, via Bella Coola, into the Cariboo country. He left New Westminster for the north on the old Enterprise. On arriving at Bella Coola he was warned that the Indian villages were infested with smallpox, and with the one sapper, a fine man named Edwards, who was accompanying him, pushed on up the valley, where they camped.[12]

Having caught a salmon in the river, they cut it into steaks which Lieutenant Palmer was frying for breakfast when his arm was joggled and the pan upset. He cut some more steaks and was squatting by the fire watching them brown when again his elbow was pushed and the frying pan tipped over, but this time he had turned quickly and glimpsed a brown body vanishing into the bush. Leaping up, he caught a young Indian whom he cuffed and released. The lad ran off howling and Lieutenant Palmer began again. Just as they finished their steaks, Edwards looked up—

'Indians, sir—and they're all armed!'

Lieutenant Palmer looked up and sure enough the whole place seemed to be swarming with natives, all armed with muskets, spears and knives.

COURTESY OF PROVINCIAL ARCHIVES OF BC

Lieutenant Henry Spencer Palmer, RE.

COURTESY OF PROVINCIAL ARCHIVES OF BC

Mary Jane (Wright) Palmer.

He knew that if you could excite an Indian's curiosity he would not act until he was satisfied. Springing up he seized his gold-braided cap and placed it on his head, and then started to whirl about and jump up and down as if demented.

The Indians stayed their attack. They gazed in open-mouthed wonder at the strange antics of this decorated King George tyee. Stopping his mad capers as quickly as he had started them, Lieutenant Palmer shouted out in Chinook, asking the chiefs what they wanted.[13]

The Indians said they were going to kill him for cutting the backbone of the salmon, which would make the Salmon God angry and he would not send more fish up the river. Lieutenant Palmer asserted that he had two gods to control

the salmon, one the Saghalie Tyee up above and the other was
Queen Victoria. He promised to arrange with Queen Victoria
to have twice as many salmon as before. The Indians seemed
impressed with this peculiar lie. They went away but soon returned, accompanied by women. The chief invited Lieutenant Palmer to come and live with them and become one of
their chiefs, taking the chief's two daughters as his wives.
Lieutenant Palmer spoke with admiration of the beauty of the
two women but explained that he would have to obtain the
permission of the goddess Queen Victoria, as she might with-
hold the salmon if he angered her. The daughters were to be
kept safely until his return. This apparently satisfied the Indians, and after shaking hands all round Lieutenant Palmer
and Edwards departed.

This is probably the story which was told in the camp
when Lieutenant Palmer and Sappers Edwards and Breakenridge returned, but it is not part of the official report written
by Palmer. Retracing Palmer's route, Adrian Kershaw and
John Spittle have found his map to be remarkably accurate,
considering that it was based on a single traverse over about
400 kilometres. At each of his 18 camps, Palmer fixed his position astronomically by sextant, New Westminster time
derived from a pocket chronometer to obtain the longitude.
Palmer's report was serialized in *The British Columbian* and his
map was lithographed at the Royal Engineers' camp and made
available to the public. Although it is impossible to know
whether Palmer and Edwards were in danger of losing their
lives, this is the area of the Indian attack, two years later, on
members of work crews attempting to push through a road.
(This was in spite of Palmer's recommendation that the route
was not suitable for a wagon road.)

Neither was the Fraser Canyon suitable, but the road was
built nevertheless. "Those who glide along through that
stretch in palatial sleeping cars of today need a strong imag-
ination to realize its condition when the sappers crawled like
flies around some of those bluffs to obtain the necessary
levels."[14] Modern travellers, moving at 90 kilometres per hour
cannot share Lieutenant Mayne's response to the canyon:

Looking up between the precipitous cliffs, the water is seen rushing through them at fearful speed. I hardly know which was more grand, the view from this spot or that further on, as we got well into the canyon, in which in some places the trail led up crags so steep that we had to clamber up them with our hands and feet until we arrived breathless at the top of a projecting ledge, on which we were glad to halt a few minutes, to draw breath and gaze with wonder on the scene.

At the time I speak of there were three trails, though they were not entirely separate. The first of these, the Mule-trail, was completely blocked up by snow; it is hardly ever open till June. The others were known as the "Lower" and "Upper" canyon trails. The lower trail could only be passed when the water was low, at which time there is a ledge of boulders along the bottom of the cliff, over which a rough path was carried. The upper trail passed along from ledge to ledge at a height ranging from 50 to 800 feet above the river. We went partly along each of these trails. When we could we kept the lower, but constantly, on coming to some bluff of rock jutting out into the river we had to scramble up into the upper trail to pass it. The mode of rounding these cliffs, which literally overhang the river, is peculiar, and makes one's nerves twitch a little at first.... This was managed by the Indians thus: they suspended three poles by native rope, made of deerhide and fibre, from the top of the cliff, the inner end of the first and third resting on the trail and the middle one crossing them on the front of the bluff. Of course there was nothing to lay hold of and the only way was for the traveller to stretch out his arms and clasp the rock as much as possible, keeping his face close against it; if he got dizzy, or made a false step, the pole would, of course, swing away, and he would topple over into the torrent, which rolled hundreds of feet beneath.[15]

The Engineers, working along these precipices in 1862, appear to have withstood the slight twitching of the nerves. Another glimpse of the work of that year is recorded in the journal of Harry Guillod, who left England in 1862 at age 24, with his young brother, George, to make his fortune in the Cariboo. By the middle of September they had worked for six months without making any money or finding any gold, and they had spent everything they had on food, which was a common experience, according to Guillod. Guillod was wearing a single boot minus its top which he had cut off and made into a moccasin for the other foot. Returning to Victoria, Guillod (George had succumbed to rheumatism and gone down to the coast earlier) took the Fraser River route, being anxious to rejoin his brother. On October 11, he reported that "The greater part of the road is finished round Jackass Mountain" but two days later he

> followed the road too far and so came to the end of the finished part where there was no trail. I therefore clambered over the stones and went along the side of the hill, climbing and slipping. It was a very awkward place, for the hill was very steep and covered with loose stones and fragments of rock which on a touch of the foot went rolling and jumping down till they fell with a sullen splash into the Fraser below.

> Oct. 14th. I exchanged my mining-pan, billy, &c for some bacon and flour, which I cooked and baked and then started and reached Yale in the middle of the day. I had to wait half an hour or so when within sight of the town, in order to allow some blasting to go off round Yale bluff, and go off it did like so many cannon, reverberating with a treble echo across the bay. The consequence of this delay was that I missed the steamer which should have taken me down the river.[16]

The Engineers completed that difficult six-mile section, from Yale to Pike's Riffle, a few weeks after Guillod had passed. The stern-wheel steamers have been frequently named in the preceding chapters, for these ships were a vital component in the transportation system during the 1860s. Although associated in popular thought with the Mississippi River, they "were in fact used more extensively in British Columbia than in any other area of North America."[17] Macfie, writing in 1865, commented concerning "the prodigal indifference of American steamboat men in regard to human life. . . . A Yankee was asked about the safety of a certain steamer. 'She may do very well for passengers, but I wouldn't trust treasure in her' was the reply."[18]

The heyday of the river steamer in North America was the 1850s and 1860s. When roads were built, wagon transport replaced the steamboats. By 1869 only the *Lillooet* was running between New Westminster and Yale.

When winter closed down the road building, and Christmas approached once more, the sappers and their officers returned by steamboat to their New Westminster camp, most of them unaware that the Colonial Office had finally made the decision to disband the detachment. 1862 "had been a year of spectacular achievement, and at the end of it, the Colony of British Columbia had a great inland highway acquired at a price of a bonded debt of only £112,780."[19] The next year, 1863, would witness both the completion of the Cariboo Road and the end of the Royal Engineers' duties in British Columbia.

Chapter Ten

1863: Disbanding the Detachment

When Sergeant-Major McMurphy returned to Lillooet in the spring of 1863, he was pleased to find his road in good shape:

April 13th. In riding along the wagon road found everything in the most secure state, the same as we left in the fall—except for two slides which has been repaired.

May 29th. 26 Chinamen hired today, making 90 in all, the white men are getting uneasy.

June 1st. The white men have all left off work this morning. They want their pay risen to $60.00 a month. The Chinamen are all at work doing well.

June 2nd. The white men are idle yet.

June 3rd. Find the men are all at work today, they found according to their agreement they could be mulct of their pay.[1]

Replacing the white men who caught gold fever, Indians also proved to be capable road builders. With the work of the Chinese and the Indians, the road was completed in August.

Aug. 8th. Fine. The road is finished at 11 a.m. this day. The actual measurement from high water mark on the Fraser at Parsonville [McMurphy's base camp across the river from Lillooet] to Mr. Saunders house at Fort Alexandria on the banks of the Fraser is 197 miles . . . and I may be allowed to state that it is finished through without any appearance or intention of slanging in any shape, the bridges are good, the turns roomy, and the grades all that could be wished. I start in company of Sergeant Lindsay tomorrow. The men are all paid and left, unless one gang of 8 men who is to commence at the terminus and drain where necessary by putting in culverts and clearing off all mountain slides back to Lillooet.

The road McMurphy built went from Lillooet over Pavilion Mountain to Clinton. The road north from Clinton was laid out by Captain Parsons, who was also responsible for inspecting McMurphy's work. Not only did McMurphy show himself to be a proficient engineer and administrator, but he, like most of the Englishmen and Canadians north of the border, was on good terms with the Indian people. Lorraine Harris, McMurphy's great-granddaughter, has written that he was later sent to Lytton to talk to the Indians there, who were disturbed about the road being blasted out of the cliffs from Yale to Spence's Bridge. Up to this time the canyon of the Fraser had not only been the source of the salmon which sustained the Indians, but it had also served as a divid-

The first Alexandra Bridge, 1863.

ing barrier between the tribes north and south of the dangerous rapids. Now this barrier was being removed. On this occasion McMurphy took his wife and children with him. He apparently convinced the Lytton chief that the road would bring travellers and allow the Indian people to trade furs and baskets. Reluctantly, the chief agreed to let the road pass, providing the white people stayed on the road, kept off Indian land, and did not molest the Indian women. When McMurphy and the chief shook hands on the bargain there was a sudden shout. Indians who had been hidden in the bush came leaping out, greatly frightening the McMurphy children.

A few miles away, work was underway on the first bridge to span the Fraser River. Sergeant McColl's explorations had led to the choice of the site near Spuzzum, and the government *Gazette* of October 30, 1862, had invited tenders. Joseph Trutch was awarded the contract; he sublet the design to A. S. Halladie of San Francisco. Massive timber towers were constructed from four 20- by 20-inch timbers sawn nearby. The wooden bridge floor was hung by iron rods from cables of parallel iron wires. The Alexandra Bridge had to be financed by the contractor, who was then able to collect tolls for seven years. (No charge was made for foot passengers.) During the extremely severe flood of 1894, the river rose 90 feet above its low water level, causing some damage to the deck of the bridge. This bridge, in use for 25 years, was replaced by a second bridge at the same site.

Susan Louisa Moir, aged 18, rode out to see the new bridge, accompanied by Mrs. Charles (wife of William Charles, who was in charge of the Hudson's Bay post at Hope) and Mr. Ross. "Everyone was talking about the wonderful bridge," she wrote. "I know it was a wonderful ride over those bluffs with the Fraser boiling below. I had never been on such a road in my life, but the bridge did not seem so wonderful."[2]

When the Cariboo Road had been laid out from Clinton north to Quesnel, Captain Grant also located a new route from Quesnel to Barkerville, to replace the existing trail which was at too high an elevation for winter travel. Lieutenant Palmer's crew was building nine miles of the Cariboo Road out of Spence's Bridge.

Another party of Engineers under Lance-Corporal George Turner was at work surveying the original lots of Vancouver. This group also made a complete traverse of the shoreline from Hastings townsite around Stanley Park into False Creek, and what is now Stanley Park was set aside as a military reserve, by order of Colonel Moody. The people of Vancouver owe their splendid park, as well as the University Endowment Lands, to the commanding officer of the Royal Engineers.

The completion of the Cariboo Wagon Road from Yale to Quesnel signalled the death of the Harrison-Lillooet route. Almost overnight the traffic fell away, and Port Douglas was abandoned. In 1863 there were only 21 residents left, and a single storekeeper, George Purcell, was living there in 1874.

When a fire started in 1898 there was no one to save the empty town. The old courthouse, the express office and almost all the town was destroyed, and hundreds of valuable relics lost.

When the road was declared finished, some of the Royal Engineers celebrated by marching around the bluff at Yale, with their band playing. Now it was possible to travel with relative ease the 180 miles by sternwheel steamer from Victoria to Yale, and the 400 miles from Yale to Barkerville. Between 1863 and 1865, the Cariboo Road ended at Soda Creek. The *S.S. Enterprise* was the first of the sternwheelers working between Soda Creek and Prince George. From Quesnel a good road ran to Barkerville. One complaint was registered by Dr. Cheadle, who travelled across Canada in 1862 and 1863. Referring to a short section of the road east from Cook's Ferry (Spence's Bridge), he wrote, "Part of the road last made by the

A mule train on the Cariboo Road.

Engineers (when L. Palmer was anxious to get away to be married) was a narrow strip of loose sand, built up at the edge by loose stones which had partly given way, an awful place."[3]

The Cariboo Road may have been an engineering triumph, but the Colonial Secretary was not impressed. Both the War Office, which paid the Royal Engineers, and the Lords of the Treasury badgered the Colonial Office about the cost of keeping the Royal Engineers in British Columbia, and in July 1863 the decision was made to dispense with them.

In May 1863, only two months before the order to disband arrived from the Duke of Newcastle, no hint of the matter appeared in Mrs. Moody's letter to her mother, but she does say that her husband "is looking very old just now, and is not quite well. He requires change but I fear he won't get away far, as the Governor won't sanction his travelling expenses."[4]

Mrs. Moody chatted about a ball:

We have been very gay lately—Capt. Luard and Dr. Seddall are engaged to two sisters, Miss Leggatts, and the young ladies have just paid us a visit, nearly 3 weeks—you can fancy that 2 such visitors have made the place quite gay—a dinner party here & at the Mess Room—picnics etc. etc. etc. The Ball was quite a success—5 young ladies, 4 engaged to be married—I enjoyed it very much and danced till 5.*A.M.* Richard got very tired but we were obliged to stay till the end—the R.E. band played beautifully, the room was prettily decorated, and the Supper first rate—[made by] Mrs. Bonson. . . . The Miss Leggatts wore white silk plain, with cherry coloured sashes, broad, rushings of the same at the top of the lace berthe, & one rose in their hair—they looked so nice. We all felt quite proud of them, for now of course we feel that they belong to *us* [the camp family].

On July 8, 1863, the Engineers were told that the detachment was being disbanded and that they could take their discharge in British Columbia if they wished, and receive a grant of 150 acres. Most of the non-commissioned officers and all but 15 of the sappers decided to stay. Of the 165 Royal Engineers and their 32 wives who came with the Columbia detachment, only 22 men (mainly officers) and eight wives returned to England. For the officers this was the sensible decision, for their pay was high and military service their career. For the sappers, the new world offered both free land and freedom.

In disbanding, the Royal Engineers showered gifts on the colony. Colonel Moody's house became Government House. The Corps library, which had been personally selected by Lytton, was placed in the Mechanics Institute (which later became the Public Library) in New Westminster. The Royal Columbian Hospital in New Westminster, a wooden, one-storey structure built in 1862, acquired furniture and bedding supplies from the camp hospital (built in 1859) as well as a large and valuable bath with pipes and fittings, given to them by Colonel Moody; Dr. Seddall's instruments and medicines were also given to the hospital. The printing press and all the maps and drawings became the property of the colony.

A last splendid social affair was the marriage of Lieutenant Henry Palmer to Mary Jane Wright, one of the daughters of Archdeacon H. P. Wright, who had brought his family to the colony in 1860. Palmer was only 18 years old when he won his lieutenant's commission, 20 when he came to British Columbia in 1859 and 24 when he married. The widowed Mrs. Palmer, interviewed in 1930, recalled that when she was married in 1863 there was

> no proper carriage available in the district, so we had instead a wagon covered in a white duck tarpaulin in which I, the bride, and bridesmaids went to the ceremony. But even more exciting was our departure from the church. The only available conveyance was a high gig. It happened to be a very windy day and when my husband and I mounted and took our seats, my veil flew wildly in every direction, while the horse sped along the road.[5]

In order to accommodate all the guests, the reception was held in the Royal Engineers' Mess, and Sapper Haynes conducted the band as it played the Palmers away to a brief honeymoon in Victoria. They returned in time to board the ship for England.

All was changing. The Engineers were departing; Governor Douglas would soon retire, and in the following year the new governors, Frederick Seymour for British Columbia and Arthur Edward Kennedy for Vancouver Island, would arrive. The bill to unite the two colonies, with Seymour as governor, would be passed in 1866, and Victoria would finally win the contest with New Westminster to be the seat of government. Perhaps there was an awareness of the approaching end of the colony's founding era when the crowds gathered on the New Westminster docks at noon, on November 14, 1863, to say goodbye to the departing Engineers. *The British Columbian* described the scene when Colonel Moody and his family, and Captains Grant, Parsons and Luard went aboard the *Enterprise*:

> The concourse of people upon the wharf was such as to make one wonder where they all came from. . . . Incessant shaking of hands was kept up until the steamer began to move.[6]

The crowd gave three cheers and, not satisfied, added two more.

> Then commenced the waving of handkerchiefs and hats which was kept up till the steamer was well under weigh and a large portion of the crowd lingered on the wharf watching her until she disappeared from view. A little before one o'clock the *Cameleon*, on board of which were Lieut. Palmer and bride, Dr. Seddall, and some fifteen of the Sappers, came sweeping gracefully down within a cable's length of the levee, which was by this time lined with human beings. As she passed the Pioneer Wharf, the

order was given to 'man the rigging and give three cheers',
when up shot a hundred 'blue jackets' as if by magic and
out rang three hearty cheers, such as only Her Majesty's
seamen can give, in response to which the crowd on shore
cheered most lustily. The excellent Royal Engineers Band
the while playing those beautiful and, under the circumstances, touching airs, "Home Again", "Auld Lang Syne"
and "God Save the Queen". In every direction, from
window and balcony was to be seen the waving of handker-
chiefs and hats, accompanied by many a truant tear. But
oh! the reaction. When all was over and the bustle and excitement consequent upon leave-taking had subsided, a
feeling of sadness and gloom seemed to pervade the entire
community.

A month later, the Royal Engineer stores were disposed of
in a gigantic sale. *The British Columbian* of December 12, 1863,
probably attracted the entire population of the lower mainland to the sale, for it said that there was

a magnitude of stuff... from a portable sawmill down to a
cambric needle. There the carpenter, blacksmith, shoemaker, cabinet-maker, surveyor, miner, hardware merchant, grocer, upholsterer, wine merchant, hotel keeper,
farmer and military man may get an outfit. There are many
of these articles of the very best description and which have
never been unpacked since they left England. The sale will
probably last four or five days.[7]

The editor of *The British Columbian* addressed the men who
had shed their bright red jackets forever:

To those of the corps who remain with us, the change to
them, in being thrown thus suddenly upon their own re-
sources, after many years of military life, is very great, and
will doubtless be trying at first... they are now colonists,
and, as such, must carve out their way in this new land.[8]

Chapter Eleven

The Sappers Who Stayed

Records do not exist to relate how each of the Engineers fared as colonists, but something is known of the lives of a few of them. Of the 130 or more Royal Engineers who remained in British Columbia (including several from the Boundary Commission), about 95 have been traced.[1] At least 27 of these either died or left the province before 1907.

Even before the day the officers left, an advertisement in *The British Columbian* of November 11, 1863, gave notice of the firm of "Maclure & Turnbull (late of the R.E.) Surveyors, Civil Engineers" with offices on Columbia Street, New Westminster, opposite Mr. Holbrook's store. The same paper ran the competing ad of "Wm. McColl and G. Turner. Land Surveyors" and McMurphy's notice concerning "Locklomond

House at the seventy-four mile post on the Lillooet-Alexandria Road. The Bar will contain civility and the best liquors and cigars."[2]

At first all went well with McMurphy. Returning with his wife and large family to the highway he had helped to build, he operated a stage stop which had the reputation of providing good food and good beds. In 1864 and 1865 he did well, but in the autumn of 1865 he received a letter from Dr. Tolmie, calling him to Victoria to receive a pension for his 23 years of service in the Royal Engineers. This veteran, now 50 years old, had earned his five medals in the Crimea. Waiting to go into battle at Sebastopol, he scribbled a note to his wife, concerning their infant son. "Train Johnnie to be an honour to his Maker and to his Country,"[3] he wrote. When the letter was brought to the attention of Queen Victoria, Mrs. McMurphy was invited into the Queen's presence on four occasions, little Johnny being privileged each time to sit upon the royal lap. One of the medals worn by Jock McMurphy was given for extraordinary courage. When laying mines at Sebastopol, McMurphy saw a wounded man lying in a spot exposed to Russian guns. At great risk he lifted and dragged the man behind the earthworks. Acknowledging this action, the Queen sent him three pounds and the Emperor of the French gave him a medal. He also saved the life of Sapper Charles Digby, another member of the Columbia detachment. When Digby lay wounded in a hospital tent, McMurphy disobeyed the order to give Digby the potion which was administered to hopeless cases to end their sufferings with death.

When McMurphy departed abruptly for Victoria, telling no one the reason for his journey, the rumour went around that he had run away. Upon his return, he found his house a wreck, his horses, cows, pigs and poultry gone and everything movable stolen. In early December of that very cold winter he took his family to New Westminster, where they suffered much hardship until he got a job as a labourer in February. For the hero of Sebastopol and the very able road builder, the adjustment to civilian life was difficult indeed.

1865 to 1868 were hard times, for jobs were short term and badly paid. In one of several letters he wrote seeking employment, he told Mr. Good, the Colonial Secretary, that he needed work desperately "to support my family as they are in a miserable state at present and a severe winter coming on without warm clothing and their food not of the best."[4] Fortunately, he finally obtained a government job as a clerk, and later deputy sheriff, and was able to feed his large family of six boys and five girls.

Many of the Engineers took up their 150-acre land grants and became farmers, mainly in the lower Fraser valley. However, behind the virgin beauty of the new world was hidden a Herculean task. The lower Fraser valley looked like the Garden of Eden but was not. Governor Douglas wrote:

> The banks of this river are almost everywhere covered with woods. Varieties of pine and fir of prodigious size, and large poplar trees predominate. The vine and soft maple, the wild apple-tree, the white and black thorn, and deciduous bushes in great variety, form the massive undergrowth. The vegetation is luxuriant, almost beyond conception.[5]

Unfortunately, clearing this luxuriant growth of "prodigious size" was not an easy task. In the summer there were clouds of mosquitoes, and the river flooded the best and most easily cleared lands. The falling and burning of the trees was an enormous job; getting the roots out was even more difficult. "You're a broken-down old man by the time you've cleared 40 acres,"[6] one settler said. The first small homesteads were isolated. Transport had to be by river as there were no roads; the land easily accessible to the rivers was also the land most exposed to floods. A road, built in 1860 by the Royal Engineers, went from New Westminster to the Pitt River north of Mary Hill, and enhanced the value of the land Colonel Moody had purchased in that area. Land speculators and absentee landlords, at the heels of the surveyors, included Royal Engineer officers.

Good land was often held for speculation by lawyers, civil servants, merchants and clergymen; Colonel Moody, the Chief Commissioner of Lands and Works, had bought, at an average price of less than two dollars per acre, over 3,750 acres. There is further information about the land speculation of the Royal Engineer officers in Susan (Moir) Allison's journals. Colonel Moody was at Yale on holiday with his wife in 1860 when Governor Douglas ordered the building of the mule trail from Hope to Vermilion Forks. Although angry that Douglas would take this action without consulting him, Moody promptly pre-empted 200 acres of land west of Vermillion Forks. "Soon a land rush was on: Captain H. R. Luard, Sergeant William McColl, Sergeant James Lindsay, and Corporal Charles Sinnett, Royal Engineers, all filed claims for pre-emptions."[7] By the time Susan and John Fall Allison arrived to homestead, they found themselves without neighbours, surrounded by the untouched land of absentee owners.

In 1861 there were no more than 300 non-Indian settlers in the whole lower mainland, but by 1871 there were 1,292 residents, including 286 farmers who cultivated about 1,200 acres (besides the wild hayfields) with 285 horses and over 4,000 cattle and 2,000 pigs, but only 22 sheep. Lieutenant Charles Wilson of the Boundary Commission had remarked in May 1862 that "Great numbers of young Englishmen are coming out here now, most of them perfectly unsuited for making their way by hard manual labour which is the only way to get on; poor fellows! they have little idea of what it is really like."[8] The Royal Engineers who succeeded in establishing farms were sturdy men indeed.

One of these was William Hall. Born in 1827 in Kent, Hall was a grandson of Lord Lambeth, Hall's father having been disinherited for marrying a Scottish commoner. Abandoning medical training, William Hall joined the Royal Engineers, became a stonemason and married Ann Bucklelow. Posted to the Crimea, he worked with Florence Nightingale as a medical aide and built stone ovens for her so that fresh bread could be baked daily for the patients. William, Ann, their three children and his brother, Sapper James Hall and his wife Jane, came with the last group of Engineers of the Columbia detachment, in the *Euphrates*, around the Horn with a load of stores, and on the voyage his fourth child, named Thomas Euphrates Hall, was born. A brother-in-law, Matthew Hall, who was married to William's sister Harriet, had come in the *Thames City*.

The stonework in the first six miles of the Cariboo Road above Yale had been done under the supervision of Corporal William Hall and Sergeant William Rogerson. After discharge the Halls stayed on at Yale where Ann operated a boarding-house for miners and William got a job as toll-gate keeper. In 1866 they decided to try homesteading and took their grant of land, building a log cabin on the Telegraph Trail near the Vedder River; the remains of a log structure, said to be part of this homestead, can be seen on Unsworth Road. Matthew and Harriet Hall took up a grant of land not far away. In the log cabin, Ann's seventh and last child, Annie Ellen, was born. It was a hard life. "When a boar slit William's leg with a tusk, his former medical training no doubt saved his life. . . . He sutured his own wound with needle and strong linen thread, using a lid from a baking powder tin to force the instrument through the skin."[9] When the Vedder River flooded their homestead, the Halls bought 110 acres on the west end of Chilliwack Mountain where their two-storey log house (built in 1888) still stands, abandoned and rotting. Ann died in 1897 but William Hall lived until 1913, dying at the age of 86.

Alben Hawkins, R.E., was the first homesteader in what is now Mount Lehman. A carpenter and bricklayer, he and Robert Rylatt, R.E., laid the brick and stone foundations of Hastings Mill before Hawkins decided to try farming at the west end of Matsqui Prairie. Having built an alder-log house, he established a dairy herd and shipped butter by the keg to New Westminster, by river boat. In 1878 he married Agnes Anderson, an Australian. The Lehman family arrived in

1879, in time for Mrs. Lehman to be midwife for Agnes, when Alfred Hawkins was born. Although Alben Hawkins had founded the community of Mount Lehman, he gave the honour of naming the area to his friend. When he died in 1903, he was buried in the Aberdeen Cemetery near Aldergrove.

Sapper Lewis Bonson also farmed. When he was first discharged, he did contracting and building in New Westminster, and then, in partnership with another sapper, George Newton, he bought a saloon. His wife Jemima promptly opened a temperance hotel and no doubt her cooking attracted a clientele. When Jemima Bonson had cooked for the Moodys in 1859, Mrs. Moody wrote to her mother that "Mrs. Bonson, my cook, left me a fortnight ago" and two months later another letter added, "I have just heard that our late cook, Mrs. Bonson, has had a fine little girl."[10] From 1876 to 1880, Bonson worked as a road superintendent for the government. Finally Lewis and Jemima and their children—Marion, Charles, James and Nellie—moved to a 375-acre farm at Keatsey, nine miles from New Westminster. Here they stayed until 1905 when the farm was sold and the Bonsons retired to New Westminster.

The only military land grant in the Vancouver area belonged to William Henry Rowling and is now part of the Fraserview Golf Course. Rowling, a Corporal of Commissary with the Boundary Survey contingent, transferred to the Columbia detachment in order to stay in the colony. Upon discharge, he first operated The Retreat saloon in New Westminster. Not until 1868 did he take up the land grant, which he named Truru Farm, a place which became noted for its grapes. He was the first settler in South Vancouver and later served as councillor for Richmond. His daughter, Priscilla, married Peter Byrne, mayor of Burnaby from 1901 to 1910, and his sons operated a logging company.

John Linn's name is attached (misspelled) to the land he homesteaded, near Lynn Creek. Lynn Valley, Lynn Lake, Lynn Peaks, Lynnmour—all should be spelt with an 'i'. A good-looking, strapping, Scottish stonemason, with a moustache and side-burns, he was 41 years old at the time of his discharge. Born in Edinburgh, he joined the Royal Engineers in 1846 and was sent to Halifax, where he married Mary Robertson. He and Mary returned to England in time for Jock to volunteer for British Columbia. The first of his six children was born on the *Thames City*. After discharge, he rowed himself to the mouth of Lynn Creek, introduced himself to the Indians, and set up a camp to begin the task of clearing the giant trees—trees up to ten feet in diameter.

He moved his family from New Westminster to a frame house just east of the creek, and there he established a herd of cows. A mile west of the homestead there was a sawmill settlement later called Moodyville, where the Linn children attended a one-room school. East of the house was the Indian village and a place where the Indian dead were lodged on tree platforms. To help support the farm, Linn had a logging camp up the North Arm, from which he supplied the poles for the Stamp Mill (afterwards, Hastings Mill) wharf. The cool, shady trail to the Linn homestead was a popular walk for the people of Moodyville. Of course there were annual floods; one of his daughters remembered the rowboat tied to the veranda when the water was very high. When John Linn died in 1876 at the young age of 54, a service was held at the farm and then his body was taken to New Brighton (Hastings) and on to New Westminster, where a detachment from the New Westminster Rifles and Seymour Artillery escorted an old comrade to his grave in the Masonic Cemetery.

William McColl lived only two years after discharge. A competent surveyor, he had explored for the route for the wagon road between Yale and Boston Bar and for the Dewdney Trail, and, with his friend George Turner, advertised for work as a land surveyor in 1863. Perhaps there were too many surveyors in 1863, for McColl was working as a toll collector at the Alexandra Bridge at the time of his death. He left his wife Ann (Baseley) and six children. Four years later, Ann married George Turner and had three more children.

William Hall, RE.

George Turner, RE.

William McColl, RE.

John Maclure, RE.

COURTESY OF PROVINCIAL ARCHIVES OF BC

COURTESY OF PROVINCIAL ARCHIVES OF BC

COURTESY OF PROVINCIAL ARCHIVES OF BC

COURTESY OF PROVINCIAL ARCHIVES OF BC

George Turner has been called "Vancouver's Forgotten Surveyor".[11] Born within sound of Bow Bells in London, he joined the Royal Engineers at the age of 19 and was trained as a surveyor. His signature appears on nearly all survey work by Royal Engineers in New Westminster and the greater Vancouver area. After discharge, he surveyed on the Big Bend of the Columbia River. Traversing around massive Douglas firs, sinking knee-deep into oozy swamps, climbing over fallen trees, the frontier surveyor risked accidents far from medical aid, lived in tents, worked on his plans by the light of a kerosene lantern, and endured mosquitoes, summer heat and drenching rains. After marrying Ann Baseley McColl in 1869, Turner became the operator of the London Arms Hotel in New Westminster for two years. Returning to survey work, in the 1880s he was a partner in the firm of Woods, Turner and Gamble, which did much of the surveying in and around Vancouver, New Westminster and Port Moody. In 1889, with partners Cooke and Innes, Turner established the Vancouver Street Railway Company, with horse-drawn carts. Barns were built to accommodate 50 horses. When he died in 1919 at age 83 and was buried in the New Westminster cemetery, there were few other Royal Engineers alive to bid him farewell.

John Maclure's second son John Charles, born in 1862 in the Engineers' Camp, remembered being lifted to the shoulders of his tall father, to see the manoeuvres on the river at New Westminster, on May 24, 1865, when 5,000 Indians came to pay homage to "The Great White Queen" and to receive gifts from Governor Seymour. The Maclure family, consisting of John with little Charles, Martha Maclure (née McIntyre, who had married John in Belfast in 1854), Sara, Susan, Sam (destined to become one of British Columbia's most famous architects) and Fred, stood on the embankment.

John Maclure, with his friend James Turnbull, R.E., also advertised a surveying firm in 1863, but gave this up to work on the Collins Overland Telegraph. Two other former Engineers, Peter Leech and John White, also worked on this ambitious project. On the eastern coast of North America, in 1858, Cyrus Field had failed in his first attempt to get a telegraph cable laid across the floor of the Atlantic. In 1865 he had managed to lay the cable but it didn't work. Encouraged by Field's failures, Perry McDonough Collins, a New Orleans clerk turned promoter, convinced Western Union that a line could go overland through Siberia to Europe. In the spring of 1865 work was begun simultaneously in British Columbia, Russian America (Alaska) and Siberia. The line came into New Westminster; the first message over it announced the assassination of Abraham Lincoln, in April 1865. From New Westminster the line was carried by way of the new Cariboo Road to Quesnel, then northwest to Fort Fraser and Burns Lake and north to the Skeena near Hazelton. The engineer in charge, Colonel Charles S. Bulkley of the American army, left his name on a river and a valley.

Surveyor John Maclure went ahead with two or three axemen to blaze as straight a line as the country would permit. They were followed by 80 choppers who cut the trees in a 12-foot swath. Next came one man who placed a stake every 70 yards, in the middle of the swath. He was followed by Chinese labourers who dug a hole at each stake. Next came axemen to cut poles, and then pole-setters, who nailed a bracket on the pole, placed an insulator on the bracket and set up the pole. Last came the wire party, stringing the telegraph wire. Sixty white men, 32 Chinese and 20 Indians, in less than four months (without working Sundays) completed over 400 miles of trail and put up over 9,000 poles. Accompanying them as official artist was John C. White, R.E., artist and architect, who had painted scenes for the Theatre Royale and designed St. Mary's Church.

When the small army had worked its way to Fort Stager at the confluence of the Skeena and Kispiox Rivers, a message came humming over their newly strung wire: the Atlantic cable was working. Cyrus Field had won the race. Assuming that the Atlantic cable would fall silent once more, work continued for some time on the Western Union project, but it was finally abandoned, leaving tons of wire, insulators, brackets, cooking utensils and tools in the wilderness. The promoters absorbed a $3,000,000 loss, but British Columbia was left with an excellent telegraph cable from New Westminster to Quesnel.

When Maclure arrived back at New Westminster, he was put in charge of the Matsqui telegraph office. Consequently, in 1868 he took his family to live on 640 acres of land on Matsqui Prairie, at first in a three-room shack and then in a two-storey house they named Hazelbrae. Beside the Telegraph Trail, overlooking the wide Matsqui meadows, with the Fraser River in the distance and the foothills rising beyond, Maclure exclaimed, "This is the Promised Land and here I will remain!"[12] Maclure did not try to support his family by farming, for he could earn $20 a day with engineering and surveying. In 1873 a school was built about a mile and a half from Hazelbrae for the three white families in the area. George and Ann Turner had taken the adjoining land and the McColl children became the playmates of the Maclure children. Later Susan married young William McColl. Sara became the first woman telegraph operator in Canada. Some years later, when Sara, Fred and Charles were enlarging a root cellar behind Hazelbrae, they found fireclay. Prospecting for a better quality, Charles found excellent amounts nearby, so the family formed the Clayburn Brick Company in 1904. Four years later, John Maclure died at the age of 76; he was called the "grand old man of Matsqui."[13]

While Maclure was working on the northern section of telegraph line, his partner, James Turnbull, located and surveyed the sleigh road from New Westminster to Fort Langley, which was called the Telegraph Trail. The telegraph company agreed to pay $8,000, a third of the estimated cost of this road, in exchange for a right-of-way for the line. Turnbull's route used existing trails. A "sleigh" road was a wider route than a pack trail but not as good as a wagon road in terms of grades.

John Jane, from the Boundary Commission of the Royal

Engineers, was another excellent surveyor competing for work after discharge in 1863. In 1865 he worked as a police constable at Derby and then did the same work for several years at Fort Shepherd, where he also served as postmaster. He worked for Walter Moberly in the Selkirks, surveying roads, ranches and mining properties throughout the southern interior of the colony. In 1874 he did the first survey of the Nicola valley and three years later surveyed the Savona district. When the construction of the Canadian Pacific Railway started at Yale in 1880, many people thought that the little pioneer settlement of Savona, about 25 miles west of Kamloops, would become the central city of the interior. Jane, now 47, decided to be a general merchant in Savona.

The stock for his large store had to come from England or the United States to Victoria, up the river by steamer to Yale, by freight wagon up the Cariboo Road to Cache Creek and then over a new road to Savona. At first he was paid by the Indians with furs and by the miners with gold dust. When the railway came through, the rails were laid on the south shore of Kamloops Lake, so Jane closed his old store and moved, with the rest of the people of Savona, to a new location near the railway station. In 1889, at the age of 56, he married Miss H. McNeill of Victoria, bringing his bride to live at the new Savona. He was a quiet, self-contained, efficient, private man, with many friends and no enemies. Respected by everyone and well acquainted with the country, he was a logical choice for the position of justice of the peace. In 1905, two years before his death at age 74, Jane startled the community by bringing into the store one of those new-fangled machines, a cash register.

Jane was not the only ex-Royal Engineer to become a constable: 17 of the Engineers worked as policemen. Jonathan Morey, whose wife Fanny was kissed by King Neptune on the *Thames City*'s famous voyage, and whose daughter, Marina, was born in the Falklands, served as constable in New Westminster from the time of his discharge until his death in 1884. James Lindsay was also a constable in New

COURTESY OF PROVINCIAL ARCHIVES OF BC

John Jane, RE, and his bride, Miss H. McNeill.

Westminster for a time, but subsequently he was appointed Acting Chief Constable of Cariboo and later yet he was provincial constable at Richfield, near Barkerville, until his death in 1890.

A number of the Engineers ran hotels or saloons, and some of their wives established rooming-houses. Mrs. James K. Keary, left a widow when her stonemason husband was killed in an accident in 1871, promptly opened a boarding-house and supported herself and her family. Her son, William Holland Keary, was to become an eight-year mayor of New Westminster. For one year only, after their discharge, Richard Bridgeman and Alexander Smith operated Hick's Hotel in New Westminster, where, a year earlier, the dance had been held after the clearing of the cricket field. Christopher West ran the Merchants Exchange Saloon in Victoria. From the end of 1863 until about 1865, Joseph Davis and John Mussel-white operated the Franklin House, a boarding-house and restaurant in New Westminster. During the same two years, Jonathan Brown and James Ellard leased and operated the Pioneer Billiard Saloon in New Westminster and Samuel Dawson and William Deas ran the Columbia Hotel in the same city. William Rowling's saloon, The Retreat, was opened after the building in 1864 of Edward Pearson's saloon, The Advance, next to St. Mary's Church in Sapperton. Either there was too much competition, or life on the business side of the bar was not as delightful as it appeared to be, for most of the discharged sappers did not last long as saloon managers. John Murray's big hotel at Port Moody ought to have been a great success, but when the end of the railway was extended to Vancouver, the business failed. He had taken up the grant of land, which he then subdivided to form Port Moody, after some years as a shoemaker in New Westminster.

Some of the Engineers lived jack-of-all-trades lives. When John Cox died at 89, he had been a gardener, a miner, a constable, and a bridge and road contractor. He was only 26 when he took his discharge in 1863, the same year he married Minnie Gillen. She had arrived in the colony in September of the previous year, aboard the *Tynemouth*, one of three "bride ships". Minnie had come out to work for Archdeacon Wright in New Westminster, but her service there was brief. When Archdeacon Wright read their marriage service in the church amid the stumps, the recall orders had already been read; John and Minnie decided to stay in British Columbia. After trying, without success, to find gold, John Cox took a job as a constable in the Cariboo. The Cox family returned to New Westminster but in 1873, when his house burned down, John and Minnie and their three sons and two daughters moved to Victoria, where Cox took part in his friend Peter Leech's gold rush. To support his family, he gardened, and contracted road or bridge construction. In Victoria five more sons and three more daughters were born.

Although two sons died in infancy, and another was lost on a sealing vessel in Alaskan waters, and yet another was killed in a lumber mill accident in California, the descendants of John and Minnie Cox are numerous indeed. More than a hundred of them arranged to have a plaque installed in the Parade of Ships on the Causeway of Victoria Harbour. The plaque ignores the other brides, simply stating: "*Tynemouth*, 1862, with Minnie Gillen (Mrs. John Cox, 1865), presented by her descendants, 1962." A few inches away is the plaque for the *Thames City*, which, in similar fashion, neglects to mention all the passengers except two: William Haynes, the bandmaster, and his wife.

John Cox was well over 60 when he caught the gold fever for the last time. In the Klondike he survived a wild ride down the Yukon River. When he died in 1926, there was only one more Columbia detachment Engineer known to be still alive.

The Leechtown gold rush, almost on John Cox's doorstep, was named after his friend Peter John Leech, R.E. Born in Dublin, Leech enlisted in the Royal Engineers at the time of the Crimean War and, after training on the Ordnance Survey, he served with the International Commission on the Russian-Turkish frontier. He arrived with the first group of Engineers under Captain Parsons and served for five years as "astronomical observer and computer", spending most of this time at the camp observatory at New Westminster. After the corps was disbanded, he joined the Vancouver Island Exploring Expedition which started a small gold rush by discovering gold near Sooke. The announcement of the new find, in July 1864, caused the first trail to be cut between Victoria and Sooke (which eventually became the Sooke Road of today) and created an instant town on the banks of the Leech River, complete with hotels, taverns, a dance hall and about 2,000 miners. Although few traces of Leechtown exist today, a monument to Peter Leech identifies the site. It is said that upwards of $100,000 in gold was taken from the gravel of the stream, and even today a visitor will probably find hopeful gold seekers panning on the banks of the Leech River.

Two years after the gold find, joining John Maclure and John White, Leech was hired by Western Union to help put in the Collins Overland Telegraph line. While working on this project in February 1867, Leech went up the Stikine River. Alone and snowbound in a small tent with five blankets, he feared that he might have to stay there until May, but rescuers found him within a few weeks. On another occasion he was with a party which got lost and nearly starved to death. They had just made a soup of an old dog-skin coat, when Indians from Kispiox found them, took them to their village and nursed them back to health.

Leech was later employed by the Hudson's Bay Company, first as postmaster and then as clerk at Esquimalt, and then moved back to Victoria as City Surveyor. He married in 1873. His bride, Mary Macdonald, another passenger on the bride ship *Tynemouth*, had settled in Victoria with her mother and four sisters. She played the piano and pipe organ, and no big Victoria wedding was complete without Mary at the or-

COURTESY OF PROVINCIAL ARCHIVES OF BC

COURTESY OF PROVINCIAL ARCHIVES OF BC

Peter John Leech, RE.   *Mary Leech.*

gan. Peter and Mary Leech built Avalon Villa, at the corner of Avalon Road and Douglas Street in Victoria, with frescoed ceilings, maple and oak mantlepieces and staircase. At that time there was no Douglas Street, but a lane into the park passed in front of the house; Beacon Hill Park was mostly forest. Mary died suddenly in 1892 of pneumonia, her husband living only seven years longer.

One of the pallbearers at Mary Leech's funeral was another former Engineer, Richard Wolfenden. A handsome man with a soldierly bearing, he was a military institution in Victoria. According to his daughter Madge, "he really was a 'born soldier'—he always marched, he never walked."[14] Wolfenden had been in charge of the Royal Engineers' Printing Establishment in New Westminster. On November 14, 1863, Colonel Moody wrote a letter to Wolfenden "to record how great is my esteem and regard for you. . . . The Government have not a better officer."[15] But Wolfenden wanted to remain in the new colony, and when the corps was disbanded, he remained in charge of the printing office, although the name was changed to Government Printing Bureau.

When the two colonies were amalgamated, Wolfenden moved with his bureau to Victoria and retained his position until his death in 1911. When the Provincial Legislature was in session, he was in attendance every day, and at the precisely correct moment would stroll down the hall with the bills to be introduced that day. In 1903 King Edward VII awarded him the long service decoration.

Wolfenden had a large family, nine children by his first wife Kate Cooley and four by his second wife Félicite Bayley. His youngest daughter, Madge, a well-known archivist, still lives in Victoria.

Robert Butler, the young bugler who captured the Indian murderer, also stayed with the printing office after discharge, moving to Victoria with Wolfenden. He only stopped working there a month before his death in 1917, aged 75. The offices closed on June 13, 1917, as a mark of respect for this ex-Royal Engineer.

Almost always present at military affairs in Victoria and as much of an institution as Colonel Wolfenden was Bandmaster William Haynes. He had been a member of the regular Royal Engineers band at Brompton Barracks in England, and had played for the Princess Royal's wedding in 1858, before going aboard the *Thames City*, where he practised the violin high in the shrouds. Mrs. Moody mentioned his other trade when she identified Haynes as the gardener creating the new garden at her splendid house in the Engineers' Camp. As it took a year to obtain music from England, Haynes frequently wrote all the parts for his orchestra; he also composed some of their music. Haynes played as the officers departed in 1863 and continued playing until Haynes' Band became a byword in the colony. The Theatre Royale, which originated on the *Thames City*, continued in New Westminster with great success, accompanied by the Haynes' Band. The band was playing at Port Moody in 1886 as the first transcontinental Canadian Pacific Railway train rolled to a stop, flags flying, everyone shouting. When Haynes was not performing, he was teaching music. He had moved with his family to Victoria where he was bandmaster for the Victoria Volunteer Rifles, the 5th Regiment and other groups. At a military picnic in August 1885, in Beacon Hill Park, the band played for marching and then for dancing, and this occasion featured also the new electric light!

There is no way to measure the joy William Haynes gave to British Columbians, and if only one name has been attached to the plaque for the *Thames City* in Victoria's Parade of Ships, perhaps it is fitting that it should be that of William Haynes, the musician, a man of peace.

Another man of peace was Charles Digby. He was one of the 30 men who had climbed the walls of Redan in the Crimea and one of the handful to survive that battle. At Sebastopol his life was saved by Sergeant-Major John McMurphy's failure to administer the death potion; he woke in the tent hospital with the doctor who had ordered the potion asking him in surprise, "Digby, you not dead yet?"[16] Returning to England from the Crimean War, he was one of the few survivors when his ship was wrecked. His brother, James Digby, R.E., died in British Columbia at the age of 27, in a hunting accident.

A quiet, good-natured man with beard and moustache, Digby took up a grant of 150 acres in Pitt Meadows before marrying Elizabeth Ann McMurphy, John McMurphy's daughter, when she was just 16 years old. Annie McMurphy was three years old when she and Sapper Digby were on the *Thames City* and he always said that he had waited for her to grow up.

The Digbys moved back to New Westminster when Charles became steward of the Royal Inland Hospital on Agnes Street (known as the Royal Columbian Hospital, when moved to its present site). Lorraine Harris, granddaughter of Digby and great-granddaughter of John McMurphy, has written that Digby

> assisted the doctors with the operations, gave anaesthetics, tended patients and generally administered the six-ward, 48-bed hospital. The operating room was heated by an open fireplace and the instruments were boiled in an enamel bowl on the kitchen range. Hospital help consisted of one cook and one male orderly. Once, when Annie was helping to clean up the operating room after a logger had been brought in with a cut foot, she picked up the cut boot and out dropped the severed toes. Digby also dug and planted the garden, filled the root cellar which supplied the hospital with the year's fruit and vegetables, and kept hogs and chickens for meat, poultry and eggs for the hospital larder.[17]

Next door to the hospital, Annie Digby managed a busy household. When a ninth child was born prematurely in 1897, Charles rubbed the 2½-pound baby with cod-liver oil, wrapped her in cotton batting and put her on a pillow in the oven of one of the two hospital kitchen stoves for two weeks. Named after the flowers blooming by the door, little Lily survived. Son Ed died from typhoid fever and George was drowned when he fell off a boom while carrying boom chains. His little dog jumped into the water and kept barking and barking as he swam in circles to mark the spot, but help came too late. Ella and James died of diphtheria, just at the time when son Donald was being born. Annie had an Indian woman named Jenny to help her, three days a week, who taught the whole family to speak Chinook. The children spoke Chinook to each other when they didn't want others to understand. John Digby, the oldest son, was often called to interpret in court. Not until he was 70 did Charles Digby retire from the hospital work.

Farmers, surveyors, bridge and road builders, merchants, hotel and saloon keepers, stonecutters, bricklayers, carpenters, druggist, constables, butchers, blacksmiths, bakers, tailors, miners, draughtsmen, printers, engravers, saddlers and leather workers, labourers, hospital attendant, musicians... the discharged Engineers performed all manner of tasks in the new colony. The work of their wives, usually unacknowledged, was often even more arduous and their "civilizing" influence is an intangible contribution. The years seemed to vanish and suddenly their children were marrying and the former Engineers and their wives were growing old. At a luncheon to honour the Royal Engineers, given by Mayor W. H. Keary in October 1909 in New Westminster, only 12 were there.[18]

As far as is known, when George Turner and Thomas Argyle died in 1919, there were only three left: William Haynes died in 1920, John Cox in 1926 and the one who remained was Philip Jackman, who died in 1927.

Sapper Philip Jackman, a Devonshire lad with the blood of old adventurers in his veins, arrived on the *Thames City*, pitched tents and cleared bush at the site of the Engineers' Camp at New Westminster, was sent to Port Douglas to work as chopper on the Harrison-Lillooet Road and finished ten miles of it before freeze-up in 1859. He helped lay out the streets of New Westminster and worked on the Dewdney Trail in 1861 until he accidentally chopped off a toe. In the

The luncheon party in 1909. *Back row (l. to r.): Premier Richard McBride; F. W. Howay; W. H. Keary, Mayor of New Westminster and son of James Keary, RE; Henry Bruce, RE; John Cox, RE. Middle row (l. to r.): George Turner, RE; Allan Cummins, RE; William Haynes, RE; Robert Butler, RE; Samuel Archer, RE. Front row, (l. to r.): Philip Jackman, RE; Lewis Bonson, RE; Richard Wolfenden, RE; John Musselwhite, RE. Sitting: William Hall, RE; Mrs. James Keary.*

winter of 1862 he was moving supplies to Yale for the men working on the Cariboo Road and in the same year he fell in love with Sarah Lovegrove, who, arriving from England on the bride ship *Tynemouth*, had become a servant for Mrs. Moody. Sarah was a slender, quiet woman, always busy. Her granddaughter remembered that she wore a black silk dust cap, and when she went out she donned a black straw sailor hat.

When he was discharged in 1863, Jackman succumbed to gold fever and went to the Cariboo, where he got only excitement for his trouble. In 1874, while he and his friend Charles Digby were working on their contract to build a trail from New Westminster to the False Creek Bridge, the top of a tree fell on his hand, breaking a few bones. Next, he was a police constable in New Westminster for nine years, a time when he was in fact the whole police force. "Many a drunk he packed home in a wheel barrow,"[19] wrote his granddaughter. He tried homesteading, ran a store in Aldergrove for a time, worked on the survey for the Canadian Pacific Railway, served as Reeve of Langley from 1895 to 1897, and was a fishery warden on the Fraser River for 14 years. He would row up and down the Fraser with a long pole sticking down into the river from the bow of his boat; when the pole snagged a net, he would haul it in, giving the salmon to needy families.

Philip and Sarah Jackman had 21 grandchildren. When Sarah died in 1917, he buried her in the Aberdeen Cemetery near Aldergrove. The grave is marked by a tall stone obelisk, with a cypress and rhododendron planted close by; the cypress is now old and the rhododendron is the size of a tree.

Kinahan Cornwallis, the enthusiastic gold seeker of 1858, discussing the Americans, commented that, "although possessing an affinity of race and language with ourselves [they] are, however, alien to us in constitutional government. They are republicans and democrats—we are supporters of a monarchy and an aristocracy; and therefore it is desirable that the latter element should be at once infused into the disorderly mass of Americans now populating the regions alluded to [British Columbia]".[20] The Royal Engineers were an important infusion of British blood. Frances Woodward concluded:

> In addition to the many material contributions towards building solid foundations of civilization in an infant colony, the Royal Engineers provided a nucleus of a society bearing the characteristics of the "best" of British soldiery, which in turn influenced, and was influenced by the fluid frontier society in which it found itself. Since the British group was the largest and most cohesive group, and as a significant portion of it remained in the colony, its characteristics predominated.[21]

Looking back in 1925, Mrs. William Haynes concluded that "Pioneering was not all beer and skittles but we had lots of fun at times and we were all young and lively."[22]

These are men and women worth remembering.

Chapter Twelve:

Traces of the Sappers

To breathe life into the words on the printed page, it is necessary to seek out what survives of the work and possessions of the sappers. We drive on the roads they surveyed but the thick, smooth layers of modern pavement hide those rutted or rocky routes of 1863. Where can one go to walk on their roads and trails, to touch their lives by examining something they made or used, to make the events of the past come alive? The list below is by no means complete, for a thorough record of the existing trails and roads is a subject for another book.

Point Roberts
1. On the west coast of North America, where the 49th parallel first touches salt water, there stands a granite obelisk, marking the Canadian-American boundary. To find the mon-

ument follow 56th Street through the town of Tsawwassen and enter the United States. The American Customs official will give you permission to circle the office and drive west about 1½ kilometres on the American road which runs along the border, past the back gardens of houses which are in Canada. On the cliff edge you will find the obelisk, almost buried in blackberry bushes. A swath of trees has been cut, down the steep slope to the stony beach below. On the western side of the base are the words: "Treaty of Washington June 15th 1846".

The true boundary line passes through the centre of the obelisk but the monument actually lies about 800 feet north of the 49th parallel. "The positional difference is not attributable to careless survey work. It results from the limitations of nineteenth century technology, and also from inevitable discrepancies caused by the initial adoption of astronomic, rather than geodetic, coordinates, and the effect of gravity anomalies."[1]

Vancouver

1. Stanley Park and the University Endowment Lands. These lands are preserved for public use because Colonel Moody first established them as military reserves.

2. The Vancouver Centennial Museum, in Gallery 5, exhibits a Royal Engineer tunic and high beaver hat, some draughting tools, and maps and copies of exquisitely drawn Royal Engineer maps.

3. At New Brighton Park, at the northern end of Windermere Street, a brass plaque announces "Here Vancouver Began", crediting the Royal Engineers with the beginning: a survey of lots in 1863 which was named "Hasting Townsite".

New Westminster

1. The Church of St. Mary the Virgin, on East Columbia Street, near DeBeck Street, consecrated May 1, 1865, was designed by Lieutenant J. C. White and built by Daniel

Richards, both Royal Engineers. As the church is locked most of the time, the best way to see it is to attend services. On the first and third Sundays of the month, Holy Communion is at ten o'clock; on the second and fourth Sundays, Matins is at eight o'clock.

The church was enlarged in 1921, the original small porch now converted to a baptistry. If you turn and look above the new door as you enter, you will see a piece of cedar board on which, in 19th-century handwriting, are the words: "This Church was built by Daniel Richards begun on the 11th of January and finished on the 20th of March 1865." The writing was discovered when repairs were being made to the roof after a fire in December 1932. Consecrated May 1, 1865, the very pew occupied by His Excellency Governor Seymour is still in the same position in the nave; the only pew surviving from the early era, it is a seat in which it would be difficult to slouch. For the first four years this was the fashionable church of New Westminster, with Government House and the residences of government officials nearby. Then the two colonies were united and Victoria was made the capital. The vicar's dismal entry in the Register Book for June 7, 1868, notes: "Douglas took away, after morning service, the most of my congregation for their new home."[2]

A hymn board in the church was given in memory of Charles and Elizabeth Ann Digby, and an oak chair in the sanctuary was donated by their granddaughters, who are still members of the congregation. A gleaming processional cross has on it the names of Sergeant J. Morey, R. E. and Frances, his wife. Although the church has been enlarged, the addition has been so sensitively made that the church seems little changed.

2. New Westminster City Hall. On your right as you enter the main doors is a large representation of the Royal Engineers' coat of arms, and at the top of the stairs on the south side of the entrance hall is the painting by Inga Morris of Governor Douglas and Judge Begbie saying farewell to Colonel Moody in November 1863.

3. Irving House, 302 Royal Avenue. Built by Royal Engineers in the Gothic style, using California redwood, this house is open to the public. William Irving, a Scot, sailed the world for 20 years before settling in Portland, Oregon, in 1850, where he married Elizabeth Jane Dixon and started running sternwheelers on the Columbia and Willamette Rivers. Following the gold seekers, he moved his family to British Columbia in 1859 and operated sternwheelers on the Fraser River, where he became known as the "King of the River". Irving lived in his beautiful house for only eight years, as he died in 1872 of pneumonia, aged 56.

The parlour on the right as you enter Irving House contains a small upright piano with an intricately carved fretwork front (made by Kirkman, London) which may have been brought around Cape Horn in 1858 for Captain Grant, R. E. Another piano at Fort Langley is also said to be Captain Grant's.

Curator Archie Miller has an elegant costume to don when he portrays Captain Irving and a uniform of the Royal Engineers to wear when reminding visitors that the Royal Engineers were the builders of this beautiful home.

4. Irving House Historic Centre, 302 Royal Avenue. Leaving Irving House, the visitor should turn to the left around the house and descend the steps through the garden to the new museum, where exhibits relating to the Royal Engineers are displayed, including one of Dr. Seddall's chests, which came round the Horn full of medicines; the list of contents is glued inside the lid. In another corner of the museum, artifacts relating to gold marketing are to be found, including replicas of the $10 and $20 gold coins minted, against Governor Douglas's instructions, by Captain Gosset. The real ones are extremely rare, as it is thought that not more than 20 were made. There is also a bolt from the first provincial jail, to which Philip Jackman wheeled the drunks in a wheelbarrow.

5. Penitentiary, Columbia Street. A sign marks the site of the Moody residence, later altered to become Government House. When the capital of the united colonies was established in Victoria, the building fell into disrepair and was ulti-

mately destroyed. The sign neglects to tell the visitor that this is the site of the Royal Engineers' Camp. Climb up the grassy bank to examine the magnificent view. On a clear day the Royal Engineers thought they could see all the way to Hope.

6. Samson V Maritime Museum. To examine a sternwheel steamer, walk aboard the *Samson V*, moored in the Fraser River near the new rapid transit station, New Westminster.

7. The Museum of the Royal Westminster Regiment and the Royal Westminster Regiment Association is in The Armoury, 530 Queens Avenue, New Westminster. As this museum is not open all the time, visitors should phone 526-5116 for information. Your footsteps echo as you cross the white-painted drill hall of 1894, with massive, long cedar beams supporting the ceiling high above. The old gun room has been converted to a museum where well-arranged exhibits represent many hours of work on the part of a devoted few. In one case is the sword of John McMurphy, R.E., who became a member of the New Westminster Rifles after the Royal Engineers were disbanded. Some brass buttons from the old Royal Engineer uniforms are there also, and a belt buckle. The oldest photo in the collection shows a rifle team from the newly formed Volunteer Rifles in an 1863 match with a team from a British Navy vessel. In the picture are Ensign Richard Wolfenden, George Williams, William Franklin and Robert Butler, all ex-Royal Engineers.

8. Fraser Cemetery, north of the old penitentiary, on Cumberland Avenue in Sapperton: many Royal Engineers are buried here. In the Masonic section, close to Miner Street on the eastern side, the tall obelisk near the old monkey-puzzle tree marks John Linn's grave. In the same area is James Digby's stone, which was moved from the old cemetery at Agnes and Dufferin Streets, and one for Robert Hume. William Hall made James Digby's stone. In the I.O.O.F. section east of Richmond Street, lie George and Ann Turner, and only a whisper away is the stone marking the resting place of Ann's first husband, William McColl; their daughter Nellie was New Westminster's first May Queen. Across Richmond

Street, in the Catholic section, James Keary is buried, whose son became mayor of the city. John Murray, Jonathan Morey, John McMurphy and Lewis Bonson are also buried in the Fraser Cemetery.

9. New Westminster. The street plan was designed by the Royal Engineers. The west end terminated in Dock Square, the east end in Albert Crescent, patterned after the crescent at Bath. English street names, numerous parks, squares and terrace-housing sites all attempted to replicate the English city. A map drawn by the Royal Engineers in 1861 shows that New Westminster as the Engineers laid it out extended only to what is now Royal Avenue.

Port Moody

1. The Port Moody Station Museum has an excellent Royal Engineers display which includes portraits of John Murray, R.E., and his wife, and a Royal Engineers' red jacket, gun and bayonet. Port Moody was founded when John Murray subdivided his Rocky Point land grant in 1882. Here, at the end of the trans-Canada railway, Murray built a grand hotel which failed when the rail was extended to Vancouver. His son, John Murray, was a Port Moody alderman.

2. The North Road. The first trail built by the sappers in 1859 ran straight north from the Engineers' Camp to Burrard Inlet, to give the soldiers an alternate route for supplies if the Americans should attack via the Fraser River. The road served more as a baseline for land surveys than as a thoroughfare; A. R. Howse (ex-Royal Engineer) wrote in 1867: "The roadway from the Brunette to Burrard Inlet is overgrown with fern and underbrush, leaving only a foot track along the line."[3] At the north end of North Road today, at the crest of Burnaby Mountain, past the part where it is six lanes wide when it crosses the Lougheed Highway, it dwindles to a narrow lane which is finally closed by a row of gigantic boulders. Beyond this, parts of the original trail can be followed down the north slope of Burnaby Mountain, a delightful forest track. Here, in the midst of the dense metropolis of Greater

Vancouver, survives a small, unmarked section of original Royal Engineers' trail.

Maple Ridge

1. The Church of St. John the Divine, on River Road between Hammond and Haney Streets, was built at Derby in 1859 by the Royal Engineers. It was later taken by scow across the river and dragged by bull team and windlass to its present location. The church was designed by Reverend W. B. Crickmer, a missionary sent by the Colonial and Continental Church Society of London, who arrived with Coloney Moody on Christmas Day, 1858. When New Westminster was made the capital of the new colony, Derby was abruptly deserted. The Crickmers were sent to Yale, where another Church of St. John the Divine was built. It was not until 1892 that the abandoned Derby church was given a new lease of life, when it was taken across the river to Maple Ridge. The glass in most of the small windows and the fine walls of redwood are unchanged from the original building, and the old bell can still be rung.

Aldergrove

1. Aberdeen Cemetery. Driving west towards Aldergrove, it is easy to miss the cemetery on the north side of the road, a few kilometres east of the town. Sheltered under a tall old cypress and a very large rhododendron tree is the slim obelisk which has Philip Jackman's name on one side and Sarah's on the other, placed there by their grandchildren. As Sarah died seven long years before Philip, the planting of the trees may be his work.

In a different corner of this cemetery lies another Royal Engineer: Alben Hawkins, whose name should have been attached to Mount Lehman, but who gave the honour to his friend.

Langley

1. At Old Fort Langley, a replica of the Big House has been built, where the Colony of British Columbia was declared. Follow the path across the grassy square to the Big House, where well-informed guides are at hand.

Regarding the piano, an item in the Langley *Advance* of July 16, 1959, titled "Sixth generation plays historic piano", related that Annie Grant from South Africa came to see the place where her great-great-grandfather Captain John Marshall Grant had been a builder of roads. Thrilled to hear that the piano in Fort Langley was his, Annie Grant sat down at the keyboard and played. Unfortunately it is not certain that this is, in fact, Captain Grant's piano.

2. Derby, the first home of the Columbia detachment of the Royal Engineers, is marked only by a cairn on Allard Crescent. Captains Grant and Parsons and their men stayed here from the time of their arrival in 1858 until March 12, 1859, and the women and children and some of the men from the *Thames City* lived here until quarters were ready for them at New Westminster. No buildings survive from this period, except the church which was moved to Maple Ridge.

If you stay as close to the Fraser River as the roads allow when you drive west from Fort Langley or east from the new park called Derby Reach, you will come to the rise of land where Allard Crescent makes a wide bend. On the river side of the road, inside a wire-fence enclosure, stands a rough-hewn granite pillar, triangular in cross-section, about five feet high. A plaque set into the stone identifies this as the site of the first Fort Langley, but there is nothing left to examine except the location itself. This spot was chosen for the fort because it was higher ground and therefore less likely to be flooded, and because the river was deep against the bank for sailing ships to be moored. The modern bank must be examined with care for it is so eroded by the river that it is like a gigantic earthen wave about to break. The various buildings of the Derby townsite were located on this height of land, in the area southwest of Allard Crescent. It is possible that the bricks used for a pathway in the neighbourhood were some of those brought from England in one of the ships carrying the Royal Engineers.

3. The Telegraph Trail. A road leading from 80th Avenue to 72nd Avenue is a surviving section of the Telegraph Trail, still bearing the name and marked at the 80th Avenue corner by a metal sign on a post; another piece of the Telegraph Trail is now called the "72nd Avenue Diversion". A bronze plaque on a boulder marks the point where the Telegraph Trail crossed Glover Road, which is the modern name for the 1824 MacMillan Portage route between Semiahmoo and Fort Langley (the Smuggler's Road).

Abbotsford

1. The Matsqui, Sumas, Abbotsford Museum, Trethewey House, has a very large bell said to have been given by Royal Engineers to the Dunech Elementary School at Mount Lehman. This museum also owns a Union Jack, said to have belonged to the Royal Engineers.

Vedder Crossing

1. Military Engineers Museum. Open all year on Sunday from 1–4 PM and Tuesday to Friday from 10 AM to 4 PM between June 3 and September 6, this museum is the headquarters for Royal Engineer enthusiasts. It is run by The Military Engineers Museum Association of Canada Inc., in cooperation with the Canadian Forces School of Military Engineering. Items dating back to 1610 are displayed. A female figure at the piano wears the black lace cape brought round the Horn by the wife of John McMurphy, R.E. Cases are filled with the tools they used and a diorama shows them at work in the Fraser Canyon. This museum also owns a rare treasure indeed, the journal of John McMurphy, but it is not on display.

Chilliwack

1. The two log buildings now located on the property of Mrs. Mildred Evans Hall, 7951 Atchelitz Road, Chilliwack (visible from the road) may have been built by the Royal Engineers during the international boundary survey of 1858. The buildings were at the present location when the land was acquired by Mrs. Hall's grandfather, Al Evans, who showed his grandchildren the site of the headquarters camp from which the buildings may have come. The Evans brothers, grandsons of Al Evans, dismantled the log buildings in 1952 and re-assembled them on good foundations. The larger building, 29 by 20 feet, possibly a residence, was built about the same time as the smaller cabin. The existence of large numbers of hand-made spikes in the corners of the larger structure, an unnecessary addition to these well-made interlocking corners, suggests that the building was thus strengthened for a move. The smaller cabin would not have required this treatment. It is only about a kilometre from the present site of the log buildings to the headquarters campsite on Luck-a-kuk Road, not a long move.

The smaller cabin contains a wooden Royal Engineer tool box, belonging to a Mr. Bouley, whose ancestor was a civilian carpenter with the Royal Engineers. The box once had a plate bearing the letters R.E.

2. A cairn marking the site of a storage depot close to the mouth of Atchelitz Creek, established by the Royal Engineers of the Boundary Commission in 1859, may be found by taking the Chilliwack Mountain Road and driving towards the Fraser River. Rounding the end of Chilliwack Mountain, turn right on Wolfe Road. Almost immediately on the right is a pumper station and 300 feet past that, still on the right (or north) side of the road, is an inconspicuous rock cairn erected by the 50 Field Squadron, Royal Engineers, from Maidstone, England, in association with the Chilliwack Valley Historical Society.

The fill for Wolfe Road blocks Atchelitz Creek. The creek ends against the road fill on one side; the other piece of the creek can be seen behind the pumper station, where a short lane leads to a fine picnic spot on the creekside. Canoes bearing the Engineers of the Boundary detachment and their supplies came up the Fraser, turned up the Chilliwack River, swung into Atchelitz Creek and so reached the depot.

3. Site of the Headquarters Camp. About six twisting, turning kilometres up Atchelitz Creek from the cairn marking the storage depot is the site of the Boundary Commission's Headquarters Camp, now on Luck-a-kuk Road. The campsite was once marked by the grave of John Saxby, R.E., who died in 1859, and by the remains of an orchard. Until burned in a grass fire a few years ago, a cedar grave marker read: "John B. Saxby, Royal Engineer. Died June 12th, 1859. Age 29 years."[4] When Lieutenant Wilson arrived here June 16, 1859, to set up his office tent, he sat down and wrote "I think this is the most beautiful place I was ever in."[5]

Mules, horses and cattle were kept at this camp. It is probable that the two log buildings now standing at Mrs. Hall's property on Atchelitz Road were once located here.

4. The Hall cabin remains, 6132 Unsworth Road, Sardis. Visible from the road are the roofless walls of a log cabin. It is difficult to imagine a family of seven in this small house. According to Mildred Evans Hall of Chilliwack, William and Ann Hall's two daughters married at the time of the move from Yale; a lean-to was added on one side for the boys, and another on the other side for the kitchen.

5. The two-storey Hall House. When floods forced the Halls to move, they chose a site on the edge of the Fraser, building a log cabin there. In 1888 they replaced this with a two-storey log house, above Orchard Road at the west end of Chilliwack Mountain. To find it, follow Chilliwack Mountain Road until it becomes Orchard Road, continuing until Orchard Road makes an abrupt turn south just as the road has reached the river. (A stony boat-launch area nearby is an excellent place to wade or picnic.) The ruins of the log house may be seen about 15 metres above, behind a barrier of thorns. An entrance drive is around the corner and the visitor

can hike optimistically up the hill. Alas! like Sleeping Beauty, the old log ruin is ringed by the protecting thorns of blackberry and wild rose, with thistle and nettles as well, and only those who come armed with a machete can hope to get through. Once through the defences, an entry into the old structure is dangerous for it is frail indeed.

6. Mount Shannon Cemetery, Chilliwack. On the green rolling summit of Mount Shannon, up Hillcrest Road, a flat granite stone marks the grave of William Hall and his son Thomas Euphrates Hall. William's grandchildren are next to him and his son Henry is nearby. In the Anglican section, at the top of another hill, is the grave of his brother-in-law, Matthew Hall, R.E., and his sister Harriet, Matthew's wife.

7. Sapper Park, a B.C. Forest Service Campsite at the southern end of Chilliwack Lake, is the site of a Boundary Commission campsite, marked by a memorial consisting of two stone posts, each with a bronze plaque. The road to Chilliwack Lake is very good as far as the provincial campsite at the north end of the lake, but along the lake edge there are a great many axle-endangering potholes.

Harrison Mills

The site of the work of the Engineers at the mouth of the Harrison River may be seen from Kilby. To reach Kilby turn south off Highway 7, about 16 kilometres west of Agassiz on the north side of the Fraser River. There are many signs to guide the traveller to the 1902 General Store Museum at Kilby Historic Park.

Just past the store museum, a road leads you over the dike onto the camping and picnic area, where a sandy beach fronts on the Harrison River. The river enters (unseen) from the right and disappears around a corner on the left, under the railroad bridge. This wide curve of the river is extremely shallow, and it was here that the Royal Engineers were given the task of creating a "canal" through the river so that the steamers would not go aground when the river was low. The Engineers sank pilings into the bottom and connected pairs of pilings with logs, to form baulks. As the current swept against the baulks from a certain angle, the river scoured out its own channel most ingeniously. Standing on the beach at Kilby, the visitor may see the pilings forming a line through the middle of this shallow "lake", marking the deepened channel.

Hope

1. Christ Church, at the corner of Park and Fraser Streets. The list of subscribers for money to build this church included Governor Douglas, Judge Begbie, Dr. Helmcken, Colonel Moody, several Royal Engineers, and at the end of the list, "two Chinamen". The Royal Engineers assisted with the technical planning and William Hall, R.E., was one of the sappers who worked on its construction. When it was consecrated in November 1861, the Reverend W. B. Crickmer played the harmonium; a choir, chiefly composed of Royal Engineers, sang with enthusiasm.

The church has changed very little in 124 years. The Bible of 1854 and two Service Books printed in 1857 are preserved; the needlecraft carpet in the sanctuary was the gift of the church's benefactor, Angela Burdett-Coutts, who also gave £15,000 to establish the Anglican church in the colony. The windows on the west end of the church have the original diamond-shaped panes, rich with spectral bloom and imperfections.

2. A section of the 1860 Dewdney Trail, which followed the 1849 Hudson's Bay Brigade route, starts from a gravel pit about five kilometres from Hope, off the Othello Road. It is marked on the folder advertising the Othello-Quintette Tunnels Park. Hikers can walk for several kilometres, as far as the old Kettle Valley Railway line, along the Coquihalla River.

Highway 3, Hope to Princeton

1. Engineers' Road. At the Westgate entrance to Manning Park, marked by a large wooden beaver, the trail to Mount Outram and Ghost Pass Lake begins. Only ten minutes' walk from the parking lot, the hiker will discover that the trail is a

section of the Engineers' Wagon Road of 1861. Upheld by a very high, firm foundation of splendid rockwork, the road curves across the face of an area of scree. This is a most impressive example of road building.

2. Engineers' Road. A stop-of-interest sign, standing on the north side of Highway 3 a few kilometres east of the Westgate entrance to Manning Park, marks another short section of the wagon road of 1861, this piece adjacent to the modern highway. The sign is to be moved to Westgate but the rockwork of the Engineers' Road, clearly visible to the passing motorist, will continue to mark the site.

3. Dewdney Trail. 35 kilometres from Hope, near Rhododendron Flats, near the place where Highway 3 bridges the Snass River, a dirt road leads northward away from the highway. A short distance up this road there is a large clearing and, at the far side of the clearing, the point-of-interest sign proclaiming the Dewdney Trail. A horseshoe on a sign marks a bridle trail, which, after fording the creek (there is a plank bridge for hikers), meets the Dewdney Trail. Although many sections of the Dewdney Trail have been destroyed, both the Snass Creek part of 1860 and the shorter Hope Trail of 1861 have been restored and can be followed from the highway up to the Whipsaw Creek jeep road. The construction of this road has obliterated 23 kilometres of the old trail down Whipsaw Creek, but the hiker can walk the Whipsaw Creek road down to Highway 3 at Lamont Creek. Whipsaw Creek crosses the highway 112 kilometres from Hope. Bob Harris's account of hiking the Hope Trail in *B.C. Outdoors* is a useful guide.

Princeton

The townsite of Prince's Town or Princeton was laid out by Sergeant William McColl, R.E.; the name was chosen by Governor Douglas to honour the Prince of Wales on the occasion of a Canadian visit. The first name of the settlement was the Forks, or Vermilion, from the red ochre in the nearby bluffs.

Yale

1. A stop-of-interest sign, just south of Yale, describes Yale's past.

2. Church of St. John the Divine, built in 1859, with the assistance of William Hall, R.E. Only a block off the Trans-Canada Highway, down Albert Street, is the church, the second with the name of St. John the Divine, built by the Reverend Crickmer when he was forced to leave Derby.

The good condition of the old church is due to benefactor Rufus Gibbs of Vancouver, who restored it in 1953, putting new wood on the outside where the old had rotted, enlarging the vestry and adding a furnace room and pulpit. The new electric lights were designed in the form of old brass oil lamps, formerly in use. The building retains its original form and appearance, for rafters and interior walls are unchanged. The magnificent copper beech beside the church is said to have been planted when the church was built.

3. The Yale Museum, next to the Church of St. John the Divine, has well-arranged exhibits and enlarged photographs of riverboats and road construction.

4. The townsite of Yale was laid out by the Royal Engineers. Although most of the buildings of the 1860s are gone, the streets remain. A monument on Front Street marks the beginning of the Cariboo Road.

5. Lady Franklin's Rock. Just as the visitor is leaving Yale, going north, after crossing Yale Creek, the old Cariboo Road turns down towards the Fraser. Follow it along the edge of the river to see Lady Franklin's Rock (actually a small, high islet). The frothing brown Fraser water comes shooting out on either side of the cork in this bottleneck. The road on which you stand to view Lady Franklin's Rock is the beginning of the Cariboo Road, the first and worst section which the Engineers built themselves, blasting out the rock. It was around this corner, with the band playing, that the Engineers marched on the day the Cariboo Road was finished.

6. Cariboo Road. A stop-of-interest sign 6.4 kilometres north of Yale reminds the motorist of the 400 miles of the

Cariboo Road, and ends with the motto of the Royal Engineers: Whither Right and Glory Lead. The modern Cariboo Highway, which carries today's travellers so swiftly and safely, is substantially the same as the Engineers' Road.

Spuzzum

1. Alexandra Bridge. A stop-of-interest sign describes the work of J. W. Trutch, the contractor responsible for the first Alexandra Bridge. Lieutenant Palmer and Sergeant McColl made the explorations for the site. The bridge to which the sign refers is the first Alexandra Bridge, which no longer exists. From the sign the second Alexandra Bridge may be seen.

2. The cairn at Alexandra Bridge, commemorating the Royal Engineers, was erected by the Association of Professional Engineers of British Columbia, an organization founded by George Turner, R.E., in 1890.

3. For a splendid view of the modern bridge, the third Alexandra Bridge, the traveller can turn off the highway to the village of Spuzzum, where a road goes through the village and then turns back to descend to the Fraser right under the new bridge. This is the route of the Cariboo Road.

4. The second Alexandra Bridge. North of the new high bridge is the Alexandra Bridge Provincial Park Picnic Ground, on the river side of the highway. At the north end, a road marked "No Through Road" heads down to the river. Drive down this narrow route to a parking space, and then walk between the colossal boulders that block the road, cross the railway tracks, and you will find yourself on the approaches to the second Alexandra Bridge. Walking across the metal grid surface of the narrow old bridge you can look straight down past your toes to the swirling brown river rushing past. A short section of the original Cariboo Road can be seen north of the bridge on the east side of the river, lower than the present road. The stone retaining wall (west bank) was probably built in 1863.

5. Alexandra Lodge. A very short distance north of the Alexandra Bridge is the old hotel, moved to its present site

when the Cariboo Road was built. (Its first site was right in the middle of the present road.) Dorine Hooper, the present owner, has records that state that "both the R.E. survey sketch and the plan of the lot in the Lands Office (Yale Dist. 6T1) show two buildings on the east side of the wagon road",[6] but as neither is dated, the precise age of this hostelry is uncertain. The building has had many alterations, probably in the 1920s. You can still have a meal and sleep in this relic of the past.

Hell's Gate

The 1860 mule trail past Nicaragua Bluff, built by Sapper James Turnbull, R.E., was a zigzag trail which descended through a ravine from the height of the present road down to a level close to the river, rounded the base of the bluff on a shelf dynamited by the sappers, then ascended by another series of zigzags. Later road construction has destroyed the mule road at the top, and railroad building has obliterated the lowest part of the trail, but in between can be found the carefully constructed trail. Park at the café just south of the Hell's Gate and Ferrabee Tunnels, which now carry the traffic right through Nicaragua Bluff. At the north side of the parking area, very close to the entrance to Hell's Gate Tunnel, a trail leads downhill to a small fenced enclosure. Persist past this, clambering over loose rock and clutching the trees, veering slightly to the south, and you will have the great pleasure of discovering the mule trail of 1860. Much of the route zigzagging up the other side of Nicaragua Bluff was destroyed in the construction in 1963 of what is called Hell's Gate Structure, a huge, invisible cement bridge north of the two tunnels (Hell's Gate and Ferrabee). Some remains of the old mule route survive, but the climb down, from the end of the Hell's Gate Structure, is dangerous.

Kanaka Bar Creek

About a mile south of Jackass Mountain, this stream tumbles down, hidden in a tree-filled ravine. If you turn off the highway into this ravine, you can find the stone foundations for the 1863 bridge and see the stone retaining walls that were built to control the creek flow, as well as a collapsed wooden bridge structure, probably of a later date. At this site the bridge construction methods can be examined.

Skihist campsite

About ten kilometres north of Lytton, this excellent provincial campsite climbs the slope on the south side of Highway 1. Through this campsite and westward for several kilometres runs an excellent stretch of the Cariboo Wagon Road, winding around the contours of the hills, through the pine forest. Though many small sections of the original road survive (the old Gladwin Auto Camp across the highway claims a piece of road), the Skihist section is the most accessible, with a good map at the entrance to the park and adequate parking. Where the Cariboo Road leaves the campsite, a sign has been erected, telling the history of the road.

Pemberton

1. The Pemberton Museum exhibits the shaft of the sternwheel steamer *Prince of Wales* and other objects of the period, such as mule shoes.

2. Port Pemberton. Several kilometres north of Mount Currie on the road to D'Arcy, a rough trail turns east to follow the powerline to the site of Port Pemberton, near the mouth of the Birkenhead River. This steamboat terminus at the north end of Lillooet Lake was surveyed by the Royal Engineers in 1861. Six broken-down rock walls appear to correspond to sites of buildings shown on the Engineers' plan. Some distance east of the site, the rock retaining wall of the steamer landing survives, and nearby, almost buried by river silt, lie the remains of the steamer *Prince of Wales*.

The Port Pemberton-Port Anderson section of the Harrison-Lillooet route, known as the Long Portage or Birkenhead Portage (Lieutenant Mayne called it the Mosquito Portage), is now an extension of Highway 99, from Pemberton to Lillooet via D'Arcy and along Anderson Lake (four-wheel drive advisable). The original road has been largely destroyed by later road construction. However, one small section, one-third of a mile long, survives at Port Pemberton, between the powerline west of the site and the ferry landing; part of the road's original rock walls survives. There is also a three-kilometre stretch near Highway 99, a short distance north of the trail to the site of Port Pemberton.

3. D'Arcy, at the south end of Anderson Lake, was once Port Anderson, the townsite surveyed by the Royal Engineers in 1860. At that time there were 17 buildings, but nothing now remains from the 1860s except the possible submerged remains of the steamboat landing.

4. The Duffy Lake Road from Mount Currie to Lillooet, explored by Corporal Duffy, is one of the most dramatic roads in British Columbia.

Douglas to Mount Currie

1. Douglas: Nothing remains of the "vile hole" where Walter B. Cheadle found "miners gambling and drinking; scarcity of women"[7] in 1863, except some stone foundations and a clearing where the courthouse may have been located. In its heydey it had nine packing and merchandising companies, three hotels, a general store, a blacksmith's shop, a restaurant, a courthouse, an Anglican church and many log houses. A commemorative cairn was erected in 1960 to mark the site.

2. Some pieces of the original wagon road from Port Douglas to Lillooet Lake survive, the road having closely followed the east bank of the Lillooet River in most places. The wagon road was built in 1860–61, replacing the trail of 1858. About half of the road has been destroyed by later logging and powerline-access roads.

Driving south from Mount Currie, it is easy to miss the site of Douglas, the turnoff (about eight kilometres north of Douglas) from the present logging road being marked only by the sign "Metals Research".

A stretch of extant wagon road exists at the site of 4-Mile House, about 1½ kilometres north of the foot of Gibraltar Hill (where it joins the present Mount Currie to Harrison Lake logging road). As one travels north, the Royal Engineers' road clings to the edge of the Lillooet River while the present logging road veers to the east. It is possible to drive along several kilometres of the old road at this point.

About five kilometres north of 4-Mile House, where a bridge crosses an unmarked creek, old bridge remains may be found upstream. Here the Engineers' road appears to descend parallel to the creek, turning north along the riverbank.

Northwards again, just past Livingstone Creek, a lane turns towards the river, giving access to a stretch of extant 1858 wagon road running to the site of 16-Mile House, on Gowan Creek.

The road to Skookumchuck village, detouring towards the river off the logging road, is a piece of extant wagon road. It passes the restored Church of the Holy Cross, built in elaborate wooden-Gothic style.

About three kilometres farther north, an unmarked lane leads to the hot springs named St. Agnes' Well, located on an extant section of wagon road. According to the weary miners tramping the trail in 1858, this was the only free pleasure in the colony. It is still a great pleasure and still free.

About 1½ kilometres north of the hot springs rises Moody's Lookout, the high rocky bluff named by Lieutenant Palmer in 1859. Although the original trail ran over the shoulder of the mountain, the wagon road was built along the base of Moody's Lookout, blasted along the edge of the Lillooet River where the modern logging road runs.

Extant wagon road also survives at 29-Mile House, but the northern access has been destroyed by the logging bridge constructed across Little Lillooet Lake.

There are many other short sections of surviving wagon road, not easily accessible from the existing logging road, awaiting the intrepid explorer.

Lillooet

1. Lillooet was the original Mile o on the earliest Cariboo Road, the Harrison Lake route. Mile o is marked on Lillooet's Main Street by a stone cairn and plaque. This was the point from which McMurphy chained the distances northward, and from which the mile houses on the highway take their names. Little survives from the 1860s except the Log Cabin Theatre on Main Street, once used as a camel stable, whose original character is totally concealed under more recent alterations, and a small log cabin of squared logs at 658 Russell Street. The Lillooet Museum has the organ donated by Angela Burdett-Coutts to a church built by the Royal Engineers.

2. Seton Lake Indian Reserve is the site of Port Seton, at the east end of Seton Lake. The Royal Engineers' townsite map of Port Seton in 1861 shows a steamboat pier, an Indian burial ground and six buildings. Of these nothing survives, but the old road to Cayoosh, with its rock work, can be found to the north of the reserve.

3. At Seton Portage, at the west end of the lake, Seton Portage Historic Park has been designated, south of the river, along an extant portion of the original portage road.

Victoria

1. The British Columbia Provincial Museum. There are interesting Royal Engineer artifacts in this museum but they are not easy to find. Take the escalator up two flights to the History display and walk into the recreated Victorian street. Go past the little theatre where old-time slapstick movies may tempt you. Facing you is a store front with COLUMBIA PRINTERS in large letters, No. 122 on the glass-windowed door. Press your nose against one of the small glass panes and look into a printing shop of bygone days. There are two print-

ing presses. The larger one, in front, is the Columbia Press (American made) which was used in the printing office in the Camp at New Westminster. On it were printed forms, proclamations, reports of explorations by Royal Engineers and various other documents. The *British Columbia Gazette* was published on this press, which was moved to Victoria to become part of the Queen's Printing Office.

Near the great water wheel, with the sound of splashing water in your ears, you will find cases displaying a number of objects associated with the Royal Engineers. Here is the block of cottonwood, about two by three feet in size, from the Bella Coola valley, with the words PALMER CAMP 8 JULY 1862 cut into it. The case also holds an ammunition container, a station pointer of the Royal Engineers, and a sundial made by the Engineers for the village of Hope. There is a replica of Colonel Moody's dress uniform. A most exciting item (not a Royal Engineer exhibit) is Judge Begbie's lap desk of leather, about the size of a briefcase. Having donned wig and gown, seated in tent or cabin, he would open his lap desk and begin the trial.

2. The Provincial Archives, next to the Provincial Museum. This library houses that most important document, *The Emigrant Soldier's Gazette and Cape Horn Chronicle*, which is detailed in Chapter Four of this book. Handwritten in the neat script of Second Corporal Charles Sinnett, who was also the editor (assisted by Lieutenant Palmer), 17 issues were produced.

The archives also stores some of the maps and drawings made by the Engineers, and many other documents related to their work.

3. The Parade of Ships, plaques set into the Harbour Causeway, in front of the Empress Hotel. Two plaques concern Royal Engineers:

"*Thames City* 1859, with Mr. William Haynes, Bandmaster of the Royal Engineers, and Mrs. Haynes, presented by their grandson Stanley A. Haynes, 1962"

"*Tynemouth* 1862, with Minnie Gillen (Mrs. John Cox, 1865), presented by her descendants, 1962"

Few tourists can understand the importance of these two ships in British Columbia's history, but those who have read this book will remember the *Thames City*, and recognize the *Tynemouth* as one of the three "bride ships". John Cox was a Royal Engineer.

4. Ross Bay Cemetery. As well as the famous British Columbians buried in this old cemetery (including James Douglas, Matthew Begbie, Captain John Irving, and Edgar Dewdney), there are four Royal Engineers: John Cox, William Haynes, Peter John Leech, and Richard Wolfenden. Using John Adams' *Historic Guide to Ross Bay Cemetery*, the stones marking the graves of Cox, Haynes and Leech may be found on Tour Seven, Section G. The Wolfenden stone is near the beginning of Tour Eleven (Section T), in front of the white marble angel on the Honourable C. E. Pooley's grave, one of the largest pieces of statuary in the cemetery.

Sooke

1. Sooke Region Museum. Twenty miles west of Victoria on Highway 14, just across the Sooke River bridge, on the north side of the highway, is the Sooke Region Museum. It contains a small display about Leechtown, with photographs, tools and explanatory signs. You may purchase a map printed by the museum, showing the route to the gold-rush site.

2. The Leechtown cairn. Unveiled on October 7, 1928, the monument to Second Corporal Peter J. Leech, R.E., was placed at the site of Leechtown, behind the ruins of the old gold commissioner's house built in 1864.

The Leech River is still staked with mining claims. If dry summer conditions have not closed the road, you may be able to watch the continuing search for gold. Some 2,000 miners lived in Leechtown in its heyday, but nothing of its hotels, stores and saloons remains. The original marker, destroyed by vandalism, has now been replaced.

To find it, turn north at the stop light in Sooke. Follow this Otter Point Road for about eight kilometres, then turn north on the Young Lake Road. At Young Lake take the Butler Main Road east for about 1½ kilometres, then turn right on the Boneyard Lake Road (probably not signposted but it is the first road on the right). Follow this to Leechtown, about 21 kilometres north. You will pass the cairn on your left, just before a gravel-pit area where there is room to park. From the cairn a five-minute walk leads to the Leech River. The Boneyard Lake Road is an active logging road, and is open only from 6 PM to 6 AM and on weekends. Drive with your headlights on. Abandoned mine shafts up to 90 feet deep are another hazard.

Place Names

The best-known Royal Engineer place names are Port Moody, named after Colonel Moody, and Sapperton, adjacent to the site of their camp. New Westminster has Moody Park to perpetuate the man who founded the city. Duffy Lake and Road bear the name of Sapper Duffy. The places associated with John Linn are misspelled Lynn. Mount Breakenridge, near Harrison Lake, was probably named after Sapper Archibald T. Breakenridge, who appears to have died or left the province before 1907. The P. & T. Logging Road, winding across the Chilcotin Plateau west of Williams Lake, passes near a tiny lake named Palmer Lake, the only place name to recall the intrepid exploration made by Lieutenant Palmer, from North Bentinck Arm to the interior in 1862. Maclure Road near Aldergrove was named after John Maclure; Maclure Street in Mission City may also bear the name of this surveyor. One of the ex-Royal Engineer surveyors working for the Canadian National Railway may have named the flag stations which bear Royal Engineer names: Seddall (near Ashcroft) after Dr. John Vernon Seddall, Lemprière and Wolfenden (both near the North Thompson River) after Lieutenant Arthur Reid Lemprière and Richard Wolfenden, and Jackman, near Langley Prairie, after Philip Jackman.

Footnotes

Introduction
1. Lytton, p. 293
2. Connolly, p. 1
3. Boyd, p. 144
4. Woodward, 1974, p. 8
5. Schafer, p. 23
6. Woodward, 1974, p. 9

Chapter One   1858: The Boundary Commission
1. Stanley, p. 10
2. *Ibid.*, p. 23
3. *Ibid.*, p. 2
4. *Ibid.*, p. 24
5. Ormsby, 1958, p. 112
6. Helmcken, *Reminiscences*, vol. 3, p. 108
7. Mayne, p. 44
8. Stanley, p. 25
9. *Ibid.*, p. 26
10. *Ibid.*, p. 26
11. Waddington, p. 28
12. Stanley, p. 27
13. *Ibid.*, p. 28
14. Reid, J. H., p. 18
15. Stanley, p. 32
16. Rickard, p. 16
17. Stanley, pp. 33–42—and remainder of quotations in this chapter

Chapter Two   1858: The Columbia Detachment
1. Lytton, pp. 291–293
2. Galbraith, p. 20
3. Lytton, pp. 291–293
4. Cornwallis, p. 184
5. *Ibid.*, p. 187
6. *Ibid.*, p. 191
7. Mayne, p. 94
8. Friesach, p. 36
9. *Ibid.*, p. 39
10. *Ibid.*, p. 39

11. Stanley, p. 41
12. Alexander, p. 8

Chapter Three   1859: *Ned McGowan's "War"*
 1. McCook, p. 47
 2. *Ibid.*, p. 49
 3. Ireland, p. 101
 4. McCook, p. 49
 5. Ireland, p. 95
 6. *Ibid.*, p. 96
 7. Mayne, p. 61
 8. *Ibid.*, p. 62
 9. *Ibid.*, p. 68
10. Ireland, pp. 97–101, and next six quotations
11. Mayne, p. 70
12. Ireland, p. 102

Chapter Four   1858–1859: *The* Thames City
 1. Mayne, p. 358
 2. *The Emigrant Soldier's Gazette and Cape Horn Chronicle* (hereafter *ESG*)
    November 6, 1858
 3. *Ibid.*, November 20, 1858
 4. Alexander, p. 5
 5. *Ibid.*, p. 6
 6. *Ibid.*, p. 6
 7. *ESG*, November 27, 1858
 8. Green
 9. *ESG*, December 25, 1858
10. Alexander, p. 7
11. *Ibid.*, p. 6
12. *Ibid.*, p. 7
13. *ESG*, February 5, 1859
14. *Ibid.*, March 5, 1859
15. Alexander, p. 6

Chapter Five   1859: *"The Labours of the Engineers"*
 1. Alexander, p. 6
 2. Ireland, p. 104
 3. Mayne, p. 72
 4. Ireland, p. 105
 5. Smith, 1958, p. 145
 6. Mayne, p. 79
 7. Nesbitt, 1970

Footnotes

8. Gresko, 1978, p. 6
9. *Ibid.*, p. 7
10. Nesbitt, 1970
11. Duthie, p. 17
12. Mayne, p. 87
13. Gresko, 1978, p. 8
14. Harris, L., 1977, p. 16
15. Mayne, p. 95
16. *Ibid.*, p. 95
17. *The British Colonist*, March 24, 1860
18. *Ibid.*, May 30, 1859
19. Stanley, pp. 47–63, and next four quotations
20. Mayne, p. 98
21. Harris, R. C., 1979(b)
22. Mayne, p. 14
23. Stanley, p. 71
24. Mayne, p. 89
25. Stanley, p. 80

Chapter Six   1860: *"Very Dear Soldiers"*
1. Woodward, 1978, p. 15, and all quotations from memorandum
2. Helmcken, 1887, p. 4
3. Mayne, p. 355
4. Williams, p. 27
5. *Ibid.*, p. 31
6. Douglas to Newcastle, February 18, 1863, Colonial Office 60, BC Original Correspondence, 1858–71, p. 146, in Provincial Archives of BC
7. Ireland, p. 92
8. *Ibid.*, p. 95
9. *Ibid.*, p. 102
10. Ormsby, 1958, p. 172

Chapter Seven   1860: *Trails and Roads*
1. Columbia Mission, 1860, p. 43
2. Stanley, pp. 85–125, and next seven quotations
3. Harris, R. C. 1981
4. *The New Westminster Times*, October 6, 1860
5. Letters, Douglas to Moody, Luard to Duffy, Duffy to Luard, in Provincial Archives of BC
6. *Ibid.*
7. *The British Colonist*, January 18, 1861
8. *The British Columbian*, July 1, 1863

9. Stanley, p. 133
10. *Ibid.*, p. 134

Chapter Eight   1861: *Lady Franklin's Visit*
 1. All Cracroft quotations are from Smith, 1974
 2. Columbia Mission, 1861, pp. 18–20
 3. Veitch, p. 115
 4. *The British Columbian*, February 28, 1861
 5. Harris, R. C., 1984, p. 17
 6. *Ibid.*, p. 17
 7. Woodward, 1974, p. 22
 8. Nesbitt, 1970
 9. Stanley, pp. 140–167, and next three quotations

Chapter Nine   1862: *The Cariboo Road*
 1. Moberly, p. 29
 2. *Ibid.*, p. 37
 3. Stanley, p. 171
 4. *Ibid.*, p. 175
 5. Deutsch, *PNQ*, p. 32
 6. Columbia Mission, 1862, p. 18
 7. McMurphy, journal, and next six quotations
 8. Columbia Mission, 1862, p. 47
 9. McMurphy, journal
10. Moberly, p. 37
11. *Ibid.*, p. 38
12. *The Daily Colonist*, 1930? (undated clipping)
13. *Ibid.*
14. McGivern, p. 19
15. Mayne, p. 105
16. Smith, 1955, p. 230
17. Wilson, p. 3
18. Macfie, p. 232
19. Ormsby, 1958, p. 189

Chapter Ten   1863: *Disbanding the Detachment*
 1. McMurphy, and next quotation
 2. Ormsby, 1976, p. 16
 3. Cheadle, p. 264
 4. Mary S. Moody Correspondence, in Provincial Archives of BC
 5. *The Daily Colonist*, November 9, 1930
 6. *The British Columbian*, November 15, 1863, and following quotation

7. *The British Columbian,* December 12, 1863
8. *The British Columbian,* November 15, 1863

Chapter Eleven   The Sappers Who Stayed
 1. Woodward, 1974
 2. *The British Columbian,* November 11, 1863
 3. Harris, L., 1968, p. 6
 4. McMurphy, journal
 5. Mayne, p. 391
 6. Gibbard, p. 43
 7. Ormsby, 1976, p. xx
 8. Stanley, p. 175
 9. Hall, M. E., MS.
10. Mary S. Moody Correspondence, in Provincial Archives of BC
11. Meyers, p. 1
12. Scholefield, vol. 4, p. 1062
13. *Ibid.,* p. 1061
14. Mrs. J. H. Hamilton, personal communication
15. Letter, Colonel Moody to R. Wolfenden, copy in possession of Mrs. J. H. Hamilton
16. Harris, L. 1967
17. *Ibid.*
18. *The Royal City Record,* October 23, 1983
19. Lehman, p. 8
20. Cornwallis, p. 26
21. Woodward, 1974, p. 33
22. *The Vancouver Province,* October 14, 1925, p. 14

Chapter Twelve   Traces of the Sappers
 1. McEwen, p. 6
 2. *A Century of Service,* p. 9
 3. Harris. R. C. 1982(a), p. 16
 4. Hall, M. E., MS.
 5. Stanley, p. 50
 6. D. Hooper, personal communication
 7. Cheadle, p. 238

Sources

John Adams. *Historic Guide to Ross Bay Cemetery*. Victoria, Heritage Architectural Guides, 1983

Derek Boyd. *Royal Engineers*. London, Leo Cooper Ltd., 1975

British Columbia, Heritage Conservation Branch. *Lillooet-Fraser Heritage Resource Study*. Victoria, 1980

A Century of Service: St. Mary the Virgin, Sapperton 1865–1965. Published for the Anniversary of the Church, 1965

Walter B. Cheadle. *Cheadle's Journal of a Trip Across Canada 1862–1863*. Edmonton, Hurtig Publishers, 1971 (reprint)

Columbia Mission. *Annual Reports*, 1860–1870. London, Rivington's

Thomas W. J. Connolly. *History of the Royal Sappers and miners from the formation of the Corps in March 1772, to that date when its designation was changed to that of the Royal Engineers in October 1856*. London, Longman, Brown, Green, Longman and Roberts, 1857

Kinahan Cornwallis. *The New El Dorado, or British Columbia*. London, Thomas Cautley Newby, 1858. Reprinted by Arno Press, New York

Herman J. Deutsch. *Surveying the 49th Parallel, 1858–1861*. Tacoma, Washington State Historical Society, 1962

D. Wallace Duthie. *A Bishop in the Rough*. London, Smith, Elder & Co., 1909

Irene Edwards. *Short Portage to Lillooet*. Lillooet, self published, 1978

The Emigrant Soldier's Gazette and Cape Horn Chronicle. Published... during the voyage from Gravesend to Vancouver Island... between the 19th October, 1858, and 12th April, 1859. (In the Provincial Archives of BC)

A Frontier Guide to the Dewdney Trail, Hope to Rock Creek. Calgary, Frontier Publishing, 1969

Winnifred M. Futcher. *The Great North Road to the Cariboo*. Vancouver, Roy Wrigley Printing and Publishing Company, 1938

Lorraine Harris. *Halfway to the Goldfields: a History of Lillooet*. Vancouver, J. J. Douglas, 1977

John Sebastian Helmcken. *The Reminiscences of Doctor John Sebastian Helmcken*. Edited by Dorothy Blakey Smith. Vancouver, University of British Columbia Press, in co-operation with the Provincial Archives of BC, 1975

Frederick William Howay. *The Work of the Royal Engineers in British Columbia*. Victoria, R. Wolfenden, 1910

Adrian Kershaw and John Spittle. *The North Bentinck Arm Route, Lt. Palmer's Trail of 1862*. Kelowna, Okanagan College, 1981

Sarah C. Lehman. *The Jackman Story*. Abbotsford, self published, 1981

Victor Alexander George Lytton. *The Life of Edward Bulwer, First Lord Lytton*. London, Macmillan and company, 1913

Matthew Macfie. *Vancouver Island and British Columbia*. London, Longman, Green, Longman, Roberts and Green, 1865. Facsimile reprint: Toronto, Coles, 1972

J. S. McGivern. *The Royal Engineers in British Columbia*. Chilliwack, Royal Canadian Engineers Museum, 1958

R. C. Mayne. *Four Years in British Columbia and Vancouver Island*. London, John Murray, 1862. Reprinted by Johnson Reprint Corporation, 1969

E. R. Miller. *Ned McGowan's War*. Toronto, Burns and MacEachern Ltd., 1968

Margaret A. Ormsby. *British Columbia: a History*. Toronto, Macmillan, 1958

———. *A Pioneer Gentlewoman in British Columbia: the Recollections of Susan Allison*. Vancouver, University of British Columbia Press, 1976

Lieutenant Henry Spencer Palmer. *Report on portions of the Williams Lake and Cariboo Districts and on the Fraser River from Fort Alexandria for Fort George*. New Westminster, Royal Engineers' Press, 1863

Robbie L. Reid. *The Assay Office and the Proposed Mint at New Westminster*. Victoria, Banfield, 1926

E. O. S. Scholefield and F. W. Howay. *British Columbia from earliest times to the present*. Vancouver, Clarke, 1914

Dorothy Blakey Smith, editor. *Lady Franklin Visits the Pacific Northwest*. Victoria, Provincial Archives of BC Memoir No. XI, 1974

Cyril Stackhouse. *The Churches of St. John the Divine, Derby 1859—Yale 1860*. Saskatoon, Modern Press, 1959

George F. G. Stanley, editor. *Mapping the Frontier: Charles Wilson's Diary . . . 1858–1862*. Toronto, Macmillan, 1970

Alfred Waddington. *The Fraser Mines Vindicated*. Victoria, P. deGarro, 1858. Reprinted by Robert R. Reid, Vancouver, 1949

Mark Sweeten Wade. *The Cariboo Road*. Victoria, Haunted Bookshop, 1979

Henry J. Warre. *Sketches in North America and the Oregon Territory*.

London, Dickinson, 1848. Reprinted by Imprint Society, Barre, Mass., 1970

David Ricardo Williams. . . .*The Man for a New Country: Sir Matthew Baillie Begbie*. Sidney, Gray's Publishing, 1977

Published Articles

M. H. T. Alexander. "It was an eventful journey", in Royal Engineers' Old Comrades Association, *The Royal Engineers . . . British Columbia*

"Archives is given sword", in *The Daily Colonist*, November 11, 1936

"Arrival of the Otter; sad disaster on Harrison River", in *The Daily Colonist*, March 24, 1860

Mary Balf. "Savona Pioneer John Jane Helped Survey Nicola Area", in *Kamloops Daily Sentinel*, August 30, 1969

W. T. Balou. "A Sapper froze to death", in *The British Colonist*, January 18, 1861

"Bee to clear the cricket ground", in *The British Columbian*, February 28, 1861

"Bride of 'Sixties tells Picturesque story of Early Days in BC", in *The Daily Colonist*, November 9, 1930

"The celebration of Her Majesty's birthday at Queenborough", in *The British Colonist*, May 30, 1859

"Commemorate Pioneer", in *The Daily Colonist*, October 7, 1928

Herman J. Deutsch. "A contemporary report on the 49° Boundary Survey", in *Pacific Northwest Quarterly*, 53, 1: 17–33, January 1962

Barry V. Downs. "The Royal Engineers in British Columbia", in *Canadian Collector*, 11, 3: 42–46, May/June 1976

W. N. Draper. "Pioneer surveys and surveyors in the Fraser Valley", in *BC Historical Quarterly*, 5: 215–220, 1941

Carl Friesach. "The Gold Rush on the Fraser", in *The Beaver*, 36–39, spring 1958

J. S. Galbraith. "Bulwer-Lytton's Ultimatum", in *The Beaver*, 20–24, spring 1958

John S. Gibbard. "Agricultural Settlement of the Fraser Valley", in *The Fraser's History*, Burnaby Historical Society, 1977

George Green. "Shaved and shorn, Dr. Seddall wept", in *The Daily Province*, April 14, 1945

Jacqueline Gresko. "Mrs. Moody's First Impressions of British

Columbia", in *BC Historical News*, 12, 2:6–9, 1978

———."'Roughing it in the Bush' in British Columbia: Mary Moody's Pioneer Life in New Westminster 1859–1863", in B. K. Latham and R. J. Pazdro, *Not Just Pin Money*, 105–117

Lorraine Harris. "'Digby, you not dead yet?'", in *New Westminster Columbian*, October 13, 1967

———. "Sergeant-Major John McMurphy RE : Early BC road builder", in *New Westminster Columbian*, June 8, 1968

———. "A Royal Engineer's Lady", in The Islander, *The Daily Colonist*, August 31, 1969

R. C. Harris. "The Hope Trail", in *BC Outdoors*, 32, 1: 28–29, 1976

———. "The 1860 Mule Road past Nicaragua Bluff", in *BC Historical News*, 12, 2: 16–21, 1979 (a)

———. "The Boston Bar Trail 1859–1860", in *BC Historical News*, 12, 3: 13–15, 1979 (b)

———. "Sapper Duffy's Exploration, Cayoosh Creek to Lillooet Lake, 1860", in *BC Historical News*, 14, 2: 14–17, 1980

———. "A Good Mule Road to Semilkameen", in *BC Historical News*, 14, 3: 8–14, 1981

———. "Trails radiating from New Westminster c. 1865", in *BC Historical News*, 15, 4: 14–17, 1982(a)

———. "The First Alexandra Bridge, Fraser Canyon 1863 to 1912", in *BC Historical News*, 16, 1: 17–21, 1982(b)

———. "The Hope or Dewdney Trail", in *BC Historical News*, 17, 4: 14–18, 1984

A. G. Harvey, "Spelled with 'Y' or 'I'—it's still Lovely Lynn", in *The Daily Province*, October 27, 1945

J. S. Helmcken. "A Reminiscence of 1850s", in *The Victoria Daily Colonist*, December 1887

"The History of British Columbia's First Band and its Pioneer Conductor", in *The Vancouver Province*, October 14, 1925

Frederick William Howay. "The Royal Engineers in British Columbia", in *The Link*, 2, 4: 62–67, 1979 (reprint of an address given in 1956)

Willard E. Ireland. "First Impressions: Letter of Colonel Richard Clement Moody RE to Arthur Blackwood, Feb. 1, 1859", in *BC Historical Quarterly*, 15, :86–108, 1951

"The King's Printer", in *BC Magazine*, 7: 996–998, 1911

Otto Klotz. "The History of the Forty-ninth Parallel Survey West of the Rocky Mountains", in *Geographical Review*, 3, 5, May 1917

"Late Robert Butler was real pioneer", in *Victoria Daily Times*, June

13, 1917

Peter John Leech. "The Pioneer Telegraph Survey of British Columbia", in *The BC Mining Record*, 5: 17–26, 1899

James McCook. "Ned McGowan's War", in *The Beaver*, 47–52, summer 1958

Alec McEwen. "Guardian of the Frontier", in *BC Historical News*, 19, 2: 5–7, 1986

Corday Mackay. "The Collins Overland Telegraph", in *BC Historical Quarterly*, 10, 8, July 1946

"Married", in *New Westminster Times*, October 6, 1860

Leonard Meyers. "George Turner: Vancouver's Forgotten Surveyor", in *Pioneer News*, 7, 2: 1–4, 1984

Walter Moberly. "History of Cariboo Road", in *Art, Historical and Scientific Association, Session 1907–8, Historical Papers*. Vancouver, Clark and Stuart

James K. Nesbitt. "Old Homes and Families", in *The Daily Colonist*, April 24, 1949

———. "Wolfenden daughter Greater Victoria's Senior Pioneer", in *The Daily Colonist*, December 4, 1966

———. "Mrs. Moody's Letters", in *The Daily Colonist*, September 20, 1970

"Officer's quick thinking saved life", in *The Daily Colonist*, n.d., probably 1930

T. A. Rickard. "Indian Participation in the Gold Discoveries", in *BC Historical Quarterly*, 2, 1: 3–18, 1938

R. Munro St. John. "Engineers were foster fathers of BC", in *The Province*, May 5, 1934

"Salubrity of our climate", in *The British Columbian*, July 1, 1863

Joseph Schafer, editor. "Documents relative to Warre and Vavasour's military reconnaissance in Oregon, 1845–6", in *Oregon Historical Quarterly*, March 1909

"Sixth generation plays historic piano", in *The Langley Advance*, July 16, 1959

Dorothy Blakey Smith. "Harry Guillod's Journal of a trip to Cariboo, 1862", in *BC Historical Quarterly*, 19, 3–4: 187–232, 1955

———. "The Journal of Arthur Thomas Bushby 1858–1859", in *BC Historical Quarterly*, 21, 1–4: 83–198, 1958

John D. Spittle. "Royal Engineer Observatory, New Westminster. Determination of Longitude", in *The Link*, 4, 1, June 1980

David Veitch. "The Royal Engineers and British Columbia", in *Ca-*

nadian Army Journal, July 1958

Kathleen S. Weeks. "The Royal Engineers", in *Canadian Geographical Journal*, 27, 1: 30–45, 1943

———. "Monuments Mark This Boundary", in *Canadian Geographical Journal*, 31, 3: 120–133, 1945

Madge Wolfenden. "Sappers and Miners", in *The Beaver*, 48–53, spring, 1958

Frances M. Woodward. "The Influence of the Royal Engineers on the Development of British Columbia", in *BC Studies*, 24: 3–51, 1974–75

———. " 'Very dear soldiers' . . . ", in *BC Historical News*, 12, 1: 8–15, 1978

Unpublished Articles

Mildred Evans Hall. "Biography of William Hall RE". Chilliwack Museum, Mss. 982.21.1

———. "Brigade Trail (HB Co.) on Eastern Half of Lickman Complex". 1985

John McMurphy. "Journal of Sergeant-Major John McMurphy RE, 26 May 1862–8 August 1863". The Military Engineers Museum, Vedder Crossing, BC

Mary Susannah (Hawks) Moody. Correspondence Outward; Letters to her Mother and Sister 1854 and 1858–1863. Provincial Archives of BC

J. H. Stewart Reid. "The Road to Cariboo". Unpublished MA thesis, UBC, 1942

John D. Spittle. "Peter John Leech". Unpublished monograph for the *Encyclopedia Canadiana*

———. "Early Printed Maps of British Columbia". Unpublished monograph, 1985

David J. Wilson. "A History of Early Trails and Roads in the Chilliwack Valley". Unpublished paper, 1982

Index